Exiled to Stalin's Prisons

Exiled to Stalin's Prisons

Albert Pleysier and Alexey Vinogradov

Hamilton Books

Lanham • Boulder • New York • Toronto • London

Published by Hamilton Books
An imprint of The Rowman & Littlefield Publishing Group, Inc.
4501 Forbes Boulevard, Suite 200, Lanham, Maryland 20706
Hamilton Books Acquisitions Department (301) 459-3366

6 Tinworth Street, London SE11 5AL

British Library Cataloguing in Publication Information Available

Library of Congress Control Number: **2018958295**
ISBN: 978-0-7618-7091-3 (cloth : alk. paper)
ISBN: 978-0-7618-7039-5 (pbk. : alk. paper)
ISBN: 978-0-7618-7040-1 (electronic)

Contents

Acknowledgments

The drawing on the cover of the book is of a female Soviet citizen who is being transported by train to one of Joseph Stalin's prison labor camps. The authors wish to thank the artist, Jane Pleysier, for permission to use the drawing.

The authors also wish to thank David Price for creating the map of Soviet Russia included in the book.

The author, Albert Pleysier, dedicates the book to his Heavenly Father.

Introduction

"Why have I been exiled to prison?" It was a question millions of Soviet citizens asked themselves in the latter 1930s and in the years that followed the Great Patriotic War. The charges brought against those who were imprisoned were decided by the State and the time of incarceration was also decided by the State. Urkho Rukhanen was arrested in 1938 and was accused of participating in an anti-Soviet nationalist organization. The accusation was a fabrication. Urkho was declared guilty, was exiled to a prison labor camp and was released in 1946. Sofia Prupis was arrested in 1949. She was accused of being a Trotskyite and a Zionist. The charges brought against her were fabrications. She was declared guilty of treason and given a ten-year prison sentence. Both Urkho and Sofia are the main subjects in the book.

In the mid-1930s Joseph Stalin became concerned that enemies outside the Soviet Union would use ethnic minorities within the Soviet Union to undermine socialism and the political leadership of the Soviet Union. Thus, Stalin initiated the "national operations" directed against ethnic groups from Afghanistan, Bulgaria, China, Estonia, Greece, Iran, Germany, Poland, Korea, Kurdistan, Latvia, Macedonia, Romania and Finland. By the time "national operations" ended in 1938, almost 350,000 people from these ethnic groups had been arrested of whom more than 247,000 were executed. More than 88,000 were held in local prisons or were sent to prison labor camps in remote areas within the Soviet Union. Urkho Rukhanen was an ethnic Finn and he was among the thousands of victims that were sent to a prison labor camp. Urkho was declared guilty of participating in an anti-Soviet nationalist organization and was sentenced to five years of imprisonment. The charge that the State brought against Urkho was a fabrication. Urkho's story is recorded in chapter two of the book.

Trumped-up charges were also brought against Sofia Prupis in 1949. She had refused to denounce a professor at Leningrad State University where Sofia worked as an assistant lecturer. The professor was accused of being a "cosmopolitan" and in 1946 Stalin had begun a campaign against "cosmopolitanism." Upon Sofia's arrest, she was charged with being a Trotskyite, a charge used often against people who were viewed as enemies of the State. Because Sofia was a Jew, she was also accused of being a political Zionist. Sofia was declared guilty of treason and given a ten-year prison sentence under Article 58 paragraph 10 within the Criminal Code of the Russian Soviet Federated Socialist Republic. Sofia's story is recorded in chapters four through eight of the book.

Source: **Drawn and designed by David Price.**

Chapter One

Stalin's Campaign against the Soviet Finns

In 1923 the government of the Soviet Union officially adopted at the Twelfth Party Conference a policy known as "Korenzatisiia" (nativization). Under "Korenzatisiia" the Soviet government actively sought to promote the cultural development of non-Russian nationalities and to encourage their political participation in the Communist Party and the Soviet government.[1]

In 1933 there were two Finnish national raions, Lembolov and Nicholas, within the Leningrad Province. (A raion was the smallest territorial unit in the Soviet Union above the village.) Finnish, not Russian, was the official language of the two raions in the Leningrad Province. There also existed in Leningrad Province 284 Finnish elementary schools, a Finnish pedagogical institute in the city of Leningrad and 434 Finnish collective farms throughout the province. The Soviet government also made, in the province, Finnish language radio broadcasts.[2]

In the mid 1930s, Joseph Stalin terminated "Korenzatisiia" in favor of a more Russian-centered nationality policy. Stalin believed that many of the nationality groups in the Soviet Union were inherently disloyal to the Soviet state. These groups fell into two major categories. One category consisted of nationalities indigenous to Russia. It included the Karachays, Kalmyks, Chechens, Ingush, Balkars and Crimean Tartars. The other category consisted of nationality groups that had emigrated to Russia or the Soviet Union from other countries. These nationality groups had ethnic and cultural ties with states outside of the Soviet Union. Stalin feared that the nationality groups were filled with potential spies and saboteurs awaiting orders from their ethnic homelands. Thus, Stalin initiated the "national operations" directed against ethnic groups such as the Soviet Koreans, Greeks, Meskhetian Turks, Khemshils, Kurds, Germans and Finns.[3]

Stalin initiated a series of repressive measures against the Soviet Finns beginning in 1935. He wanted to secure the border regions of the Soviet Union with Finland and Estonia by creating military zones from which all non-Russians would be expelled on grounds that they were politically unreliable. On March 25, 1935, Genrikh Yagoda, head of the NKVD, (see Glossary- Soviet secret police) reported on the proposed removal of "anti-Soviet elements" from Karelia and the Leningrad Province.[4] (Yagoda oversaw the development of a vast network of prison labor camps, prison labor colonies and special settlements.) Although Yagoda's report made no reference to nationalities, many of the "anti-Soviet elements" were ethnic Finns. Yagoda's report specified that the NKVD would remove 3,547 families living within 22 kilometers (13.5 miles) of the Soviet Union's borders with Finland and Estonia. This was to be done between April 1 and April 25 of 1935. Yagoda instructed the NKVD to exile 1,700 families to Tadzhikistan, 316 families to western Siberia and 1,536 families to Kazakhstan. Yagoda's report noted that the NKVD was not to deport former Red partisans, family members of Red Army soldiers, tradesmen and foreign passport holders. Of the more than 3,000 families that were removed, close to 2,000 families (7,000 people) were ethnic Finns.[5]

In 1937, Stalin's regime abolished the Finnish national raions in the Leningrad Province. The cultural institutions within these raions did not survive long without administrative support. Between 1937 and 1938 Stalin's government shut down all of the Finnish-language publishing houses, the schools administered in Finnish, the Finnish-language radio broadcasts and the churches in which worship services were conducted in the Finnish language.[6]

In 1938, the regime of Stalin took action against spies and diversionists. The State viewed anybody with a foreign sounding name as a potential spy or a diversionist. On January 31, 1938, Nikolai Yezhov issued a memorandum to the Central Committee of the Communist Party regarding a Politburo decision which was to extend, until April 18, 1938, a NKVD operation to neutralize spies and diversionists.[7] (Yezhov, at this time, was the head of the NKVD. Earlier, on September 25, 1936, Stalin had sent a telegram from Sochi to Moscow informing the members of the Politburo that Yagoda was to be removed as head of the NKVD. The man who would take his place was Yezhov.)

The report that was sent to the Central Committee by Yezhov specifically listed eleven suspect nationalities that were to be included in the NKVD operation. The nationalities were the Finns, Latvians, Estonians, Poles, Germans, Greeks, Iranians, Chinese, Romanians, Macedonians and Bulgarians. The NKVD operation did not distinguish between Soviet citizens and foreign passport holders; ethnicity was the determining factor in identifying loyalty to the Soviet Union.[8] During the length of the operation, the NKVD arrested a large number of Soviet Finns. From January 1, 1938, to January 1, 1939, the number of soviet Finns being held in prison labor camps increased from 997 to 2,371.[9]

Urkho Rukhanen, an ethnic Finn, was arrested on June 26, 1938. He was accused of participating in a counter-revolutionary organization and was brought to one of the prisons in the city of Leningrad. Here he was interrogated by agents of the NKVD. (see Glossary-Soviet secret police) After a period of time, Urkho was moved to "Kresty" prison, Leningrad's most famous prison. (see Glossary-Kresty) Urkho would be detained in three prisons at different times in Leningrad during a period of seventeen months before he was finally transported to a prison labor camp. The State had decided that Urkho was guilty of participating in an anti-Soviet nationalist organization. His prison sentence was five years but the sentence would be extended by more than three years. Urkho was released in August 1946.

The following chapter is a record of Urkho's recollections. The chapter begins with Urkho recounting the events leading up to his arrest. Thereafter, he describes the treatment to which he was subjected while he was detained in Leningrad's prisons. After Urkho was sentenced, he was transported by train to Tavda. The chapter concludes with Urkho's description of life in the prison labor camp and his eventual release.

NOTES

1. J. Otto Pohl, Ethnic Cleansing in the USSR, 1937–1949 (Westport, Connecticut: Greenwood Press, 1999), 3.
2. Pohl, Ethnic Cleansing in the USSR, 1937–1949, 22.
3. Pohl, Ethnic Cleansing in the USSR, 1937–1949, 4.
4. Pohl, Ethnic Cleansing in the USSR, 1937–1949, 22.
5. Pohl, Ethnic Cleansing in the USSR, 1937–1949, 23.
6. Pohl, Ethnic Cleansing in the USSR, 1937–1949, 23.
7. Pohl, Ethnic Cleansing in the USSR, 1937–1949, 23.
8. Pohl, Ethnic Cleansing in the USSR, 1937–1949, 23.
9. Pohl, Ethnic Cleansing in the USSR, 1937–1949, 23.

Chapter Two

Urkho Rukhanen

Arrested and Exiled

Urkho Rukhanen was born on June 30, 1907, in Lamposaari, Finland. In 1913, Urkho's father traveled to Russia in search of employment. He would bring his family to Nevskaya Dubrovka, located not far from St. Petersburg, after he acquired a job in a woodworking factory. In Nevskaya Dubrovka, Urkho would attend school in which the subject matter was presented in the Finnish language. In 1922, Urkho was sent to Petrozavodsk to attend a pedagogical vocational school and upon his graduation he was hired to teach at the school. (The community of Petrozavodsk had a predominantly Finnish population. In 1922 Petrozavodsk was located in an area called Karelia. In 1923, the Russian part of Karelia became the Karelian Autonomous Soviet Socialist Republic of the Soviet Union and Petrozavodsk would become an important city within the newly created republic.)

In 1928, Urkho moved to Leningrad to attend a newly established school of Finnish studies within the Leningrad State Pedagogical Institute. As a student at the institute, Urkho participated in the cultural affairs of Leningrad's Finns. He was one of several editors of the *Nouri Kaarti*, a newspaper published in the Finnish language. While attending the institute, Urkho married Lilya who was also Finnish and she too was a student at the institute. Following their graduation from the institute, Lilya worked as a teacher and Urkho began taking post graduate courses. The year was 1931. In the following year, Lilya gave birth to a son who would die from tuberculosis a year later. A second son was born in August 1933, and he was given the name Reima. Five months later, in December, 1933, Urkho moved to Petrozavodsk. He had been hired by the newly created Karelian Pedagogical Institute as a professor of Finnish and Western literature.

Figure 2.1. Urkho Rukhanen in his later years. *Source:* Drawing by Jane Pleysier.

Several years later Urkho was arrested and brought to one of the prisons in the city of Leningrad. He was accused of participating in a counterrevolutionary organization. Following a number of interrogations, Urkho was moved to Kresty, Leningrad's most famous prison. Urkho would be detained in three prisons during a period of seventeen months before he was finally transported east to a prison labor camp located in Tavda (a town in the east part of Sverdlovskaya Province in Western Siberia). The State had decided that Urkho was guilty of participating in an anti-Soviet nationalist organization. His prison sentence was five years but the sentence would be extended by more than three years. Urkho was released in August 1946.

URKHO'S RECOLLECTIONS

In the following paragraphs, Urkho recounts his arrest, the interrogations to which he was subjected while he was being detained in Leningrad, the life that he experienced after he was exiled to a prison labor camp in Tavda and his release from the prison camp:

Lilya and I went to Krasnogvardeisk after she finished her spring semester. In Krasnogvardeisk the husband of Lilya's sister [the husband's name was Fyodor] took me aside and whispered: "Listen, Urkho, last evening some officials [NKVD officers] approached me and asked about you. They warned me not to tell anyone about their inquiry about you."

What could I do in this situation, disappear? But I had not committed a crime. If I did go into hiding the authorities would know that Fyodor, my brother-in-law, had alerted me. And he would more than likely be arrested. I told Fyodor to go to the store and bring back a bottle of vodka—it was the only cure for the sickening feeling that I suddenly felt within me.

The next day Lilya and I traveled to Nevskaya Dubrovka to visit my parents. A week went by but no one approached me. Sunday, June 26, 1938, was Election Day in the Soviet Union; all citizens who were registered to vote were expected to vote and elect deputies to the Supreme Council. I was registered in Krasnogvardeisk which meant that I had to return to Krasnogvardeisk. Lilya and I agreed that we would meet in Leningrad after the elections.

Before leaving, I packed a small suitcase with some underwear, a towel, a bar of soap and a toothbrush. [These were items that Urkho would need if he were arrested and incarcerated.]Yet, I did not think that I would be arrested while performing my duty as a citizen. I assumed that the men who were looking for me expected me to do my civic duty; they expected me to vote in Krasnogvardeisk.

When I arrived in Gatchina [Urkho used the name Gatchina instead of Krasnogvardeisk], I immediately made my way to the voting station. I showed the officer at the voting station my passport [internal passport], but he could not find my name in the list of citizens who were registered in the district. He advised me to go and talk to the chairman of the election commission. I left and went to see the chairman who asked me to wait while he went to the telephone. When he returned, he asked me to wait again. After a short while two men appeared in civilian clothes. I recognized one of them; it was our [apartment] groundskeeper. I knew that the men had come to arrest me. Nevertheless, I completed my civic duty; I handed in my marked voting ballot and left the room. As I was walking down the stairs of the voting station, someone placed his hand on my shoulder and asked, "Are you Rukhanen?" "Yes, I am," I replied. "The car is waiting, please get in."

I was brought to a police station. In the station, I was held behind a small barricade and standing in front of it was a policeman who was on duty. Late that night, I was brought to a room which was being used as a temporary holding cell for men who had recently been arrested. The majority of them were hooligans and small time thieves. They were rather friendly towards me and offered me the best sleeping place in the room. I laid down my coat on the plank bed, used my small suitcase as a pillow and tried to sleep. In the morning, each of us was given a piece of bread and we all shared one large bowl of soup. After breakfast, we were told to get ready to go. There were fifteen of us.

We were led as one group through the streets of Gatchina by armed guards with German shepherd dogs. It was embarrassing and I hoped that my colleagues and students would not see me in this predicament. Fortunately, I did not see anyone that I knew and finally we arrived at the Tatyanino railway station [not far from the town of Pushkin].

After a short while, the passenger train which was to transport us to our next destination arrived at the station. We were placed in one of the cars and in the car, I saw a former acquaintance. His name was Kinnary or Skinnary. He was a school teacher and an Ingermanland Finn. He was sitting by a window and I could hear him whisper as he looked out: "Good-bye house, good-bye dear wife and children, good-bye forests and villages; I shall never see you again." I could see tears falling from his eyes.

When we arrived in Leningrad we were marched to a distant corner of the Varshavskiy railway station. After about an hour, a "Black Raven" arrived to bring us to a prison. (Black Raven was the name given to a vehicle used by the NKVD to transport a person who was under arrest. The vehicle was painted black.) I was brought to a prison on Voinova Street. There they took my finger prints as if I were a criminal. Then I was brought to a huge unoccupied cell. It was while I was alone in the cell that I began to realize the seriousness of my situation.

That evening, another prisoner was brought into the cell. He was older. He was a Pole and his name was Yasinskiy. He had already served time in the famous prison named "Kresty." (Kresty, built in 1884–1892, was the most famous prison in St. Petersburg, Petrograd and Leningrad. Eight of the buildings form architecturally two crosses and thus the prison was named Kresty which is translated "Crosses" in Russian.) Yasinskiy was optimistic about his future. He said his arrest was nothing but a terrible mistake. He believed that the truth inevitably would be revealed and acknowledged and he would be released.

In the morning a guard arrived and announced: "Rukhanen, lets go and take your belongings." It wasn't until later that I understood the meaning of the announcement. The guard meant that I was going on a journey.

The guard brought me to another large cell. One of the walls of the cell was made of metal bars woven together in a latticed design. Through the latticed design a prison guard was able to see the prisoners and watch their actions. It was a design that dated back to tsarist Russia. During [Nikolai] Yezhov's time they added an "improvement." A long curtain was hung in front of the latticed barrier so that the prisoners inside the cell could not see the guards who were walking past their cell, yet the guards could still see the prisoners. Large box-shaped sconces, made of wood, were also placed on the outside of the prison windows. The sconces allowed the daylight to enter the prison cell but prevented the prisoners from seeing the outdoors except for a small piece of the sky.

Vladimir Shmidtgoff, the Soviet poet, was incarcerated in "Kresty." The words of one of his poems had earlier been put to music and it became a popular song sung by the Young Pioneers. "Oh, how nice it is to live in the Soviet nation!" From his cell in "Kresty," Shmidtgoff was able to hear a group of Young Pioneers singing his song as they marched past the prison. However, due to the wooden sconces placed on the outside of the windows he was unable to see the marching Young Pioneers. (see Glossary—Young Pioneers)

The large cell to which I was brought was overcrowded with prisoners. There were some one hundred prisoners in the room. Some of the men were sitting on piles of stacked wooden pallets. Other men were walking forth and back in their underwear. In one corner of the room there was a primitive "washroom" separated from the rest of the room by a small wall that was no higher than four feet. The person who relieved himself in the toilet could not be seen by the other prisoners as he sat down but the sounds that he made could be heard and the odor of the human waste permeated the room.

I was astonished that so many people could fit into one cell room. It was one of many cells in the prison and the prison was one of several in Leningrad. Who knows how many prisons there were in the Soviet Union? Whenever a group of prisoners was sent to another location, a new group of prisoners was brought in almost immediately. Among the prisoners, there were engineers, students, teachers, writers, physicians, factory workers, members of collective farms, actors, scientists and Communist Party leaders. Every social group was represented by the prisoners. Even men who had been awarded by the Party for their outstanding work were arrested and sent to prison. It happened to the director of a large mill in Leningrad named the "Bolshevik." He had been awarded the Order of Lenin but when he arrived in prison, the Order of Lenin was torn from his jacket. The prison guard told him: "You won't need this any more." (see Glossary—Order of Lenin)

There was the constant sound of many voices in the cell and the room was full of tobacco smoke. Towards evening, the prison guard ordered us to lie down and sleep. We placed some of the pallets on wooden trestles and by doing so we created two level plank beds. The plank beds were large enough to sleep on but they were uncomfortable. We undressed and used our clothes as blankets. My bed was near where Aatu Khyamyalainen was sleeping. Aatu was a teacher. I knew Aatu because we had studied together in Leningrad Pedagogical Institute.

As I was about to fall asleep, I heard a prison guard yell: "Rukhanen! Go to the preliminary investigator." I climbed off my plank bed and put on my clothes. As I left the room, the guard ordered me to place my hands behind my back.

The corridor that we walked down was long and it had many turns and staircases going up and down. Whenever we were approached by another prisoner who was also being led by a guard, I was ordered to stop and face the wall.

Near the door of the preliminary investigator's room there was a booth [shaped like a telephone booth]. I was told to stand in the booth and wait. I had waited a long time when I was finally ordered to enter the preliminary investigator's room.

The preliminary investigator was a young thin man. He was sitting at a table. A distance from the table there was a chair and I was told to sit on the chair. He asked me my first name, my last name and the date and place of my birth. He asked if I had relatives who lived outside of the Soviet Union and if I was a member of the Communist Party or if I was a Komsomol member. (see Glossary—Komsomol) He then wanted the names of my relatives, my friends and other people who were acquaintances. I decided to name only those people who would be complimentary towards me. I referred to Tikhomirov, Bazanov and someone else. [Tikhomirov and Bazanov are Russian names.]

The investigator added: "Guttary, Yakkola, Khusu" [Finnish names].

"Why do you ask, if you already know?" I retorted. "Where did you come by these names?"

"Shut up and don't lie! Look at this photo!"

"What photo, comrade investigator?"

"I am not your comrade! Look, you are in this photo!"

Then I remembered. At the end of May, I had traveled to Petrozavodsk to bury my sister, Matti Khusu. On one of the Sundays, Guttary,Yakkola, Khusu and I made a trip with our families to Lososinka and it was Guttary who had taken the photograph. I suppose they (the NKVD) found the photograph in my sister's apartment; there was no other way for them to have gotten the photograph.

"And now," the investigator continued, "tell me about your counter- revolutionary activities."

At that moment a security guard (a strong individual who had the appearance of a bouncer) appeared at the door of the room.

I told the investigator that I was a professor of Finnish literature at the university, that I wrote text books used by students and that I carried out all of my responsibilities to the Communist Party of the Soviet Union.

"Why are you telling me fairy tales and why are you sitting here as if you are an honest guest? Stand up! Tell the truth! Which foreign state do you work for?"

"I am sorry but I do not know what you are talking about."

"Don't lie to me! We know that you and your people are planning to move the borderline that exists between Finland and the Soviet Union." [The investigator was implying that Urkho and his fellow Finns wanted to repossess territory that the Soviet Union had taken from Finland.]

The investigator's claim was absolute nonsense so I responded with somewhat of a smile. The security guard noticed this and he immediately came forward and struck me in the head near my ear and then he kicked me in the groin. "This will teach you to laugh at us," he said, "you son of a bitch."

Shortly thereafter the security guard left and the investigator began writing his report. He wrote for quite a while and when he finished he ordered me to read the report and sign it.

The report included a description of a counterrevolutionary organization and of my participation in the organization.

"I will not sign the report," I told him. "All of this is nothing but nonsense."

I had read about organizations of spies and "people's enemies" in our Soviet newspapers and I was aware that the people who were accused of participating in these organizations were put to death. I was sure that they were going to execute me.

"Stop complaining, you son of a bitch. Sign it!"

"You know of course that the organization you have described in your report does not exist because you invented it. Who needs this kind of fiction? Or maybe the new Constitution of the Soviet Union has given you the right to charge me with false accusations?"

The investigator reacted to my comments by grabbing a thick book from his table and striking me in the head with it. "This is your Constitution," he yelled.

He then sat down. He put his head in his hands and seemed to be nodding. But suddenly he jumped up and yelled: "Are you going to sign it you f____ agent?"

"No, I will not sign it. You may do to me whatever you want but I will not sign it"

He then jumped up, grabbed my head and beat it against the wall and again repeated the question. But again he got the same answer.

Tired and angry, he finally called for a guard to bring me to my cell. But before I left the room, he murmured that in time I would sign the report.

I shared a cell with Yasinskiy, the Pole, who I had met earlier. He too would be interrogated several days later and after he was brought back he could hardly stand due to the terrible beating to which he had been subjected. He showed me his back—it was covered with blood.

Yasinskiy had refused to sign a form which listed the names of Red Army military commanders who were being accused of betraying the Motherland. Yasinskiy's son was among the names that were listed. [Yasinskiy's signature would be used to confirm the accusation.]

Later Yasinskiy was called out of the cell again and when he was brought back in the morning, he was unable to hear. The beating that he suffered had caused him to lose his hearing. He was sent to the prison hospital. I would never see him again.

I remember an old clever lawyer by the name of Neliubin. He was a Bolshevik who had joined the Bolsheviks back in 1906. I was told that when he appeared before the preliminary investigator he was asked why he had joined (infiltrated) the Communist Party. The old Bolshevik replied: "You nonentity! What do you know about the Party? While you were still crawling on your hands and knees under the table, I helped create the Party and I stormed the Winter Palace [to remove the Provisional Government]."

"Don't brag to me," the investigator interrupted, "we will force you to haul shit on your back."

One night I was awakened by Aatu Khyamyalainen [Finnish name].

"Listen, Urkho I want to tell you something terrible."

"I want to sleep," I told Aatu, "tell me in the morning."

"No, listen! I was called before two preliminary investigators. They asked me if I knew Yuho Kaivyaryainen [Finnish name]. I said that I did know Yuho. They then demanded that I confirm that he [Yuho] was a member of a counterrevolutionary organization. They told me that all I needed to do was sign a document that they would prepare and nothing more. I refused. They began yelling at me using foul language and warning me that my fate was in my own hands. A guard then brought Yuho into the room. The investigators asked me if I knew him. I replied that I did. They asked Yuho if he knew me. He said, 'Yes.' They then asked several meaningless questions and then one of the investigators began writing a statement. When he finished the statement, he read it out loud. It accused Yuho and me of being members of the same counterrevolutionary organization. It claimed that we were in the organization together. The investigators ordered me to sign the statement. I had no choice but to sign it. They then ordered Yuho to come to the table and sign the statement as well. Yuho took the paper and ripped it up. The investigators grabbed Yuho and tied him up. Thereafter, they drafted a new statement and ordered me to sign it. I signed it but as I did Yuho yelled at me calling me a bastard and lowlife. The investigators did not order Yuho to sign the statement because they knew he would rip it up. They instead called for a prison guard and he escorted me to our cell. I don't know what happened to Yuho."

Towards the end of August a guard appeared at the door of the cell and yelled "Sulander, Khyamyalainen and Rukhanen—let's go and take your belongings."

We were escorted to a larger prison cell. It was already crowded but still more prisoners were being forced into the room. It was so crowded that there was no room to sit down. The men smoked and talked to each other standing up. Most of the conversations were conducted in Finnish. Khyamyalainen was standing next to me when suddenly he whispered, "Look, Yuho is in here also. Please tell him that I was forced to sign the statement [drafted by the investigators]."

Yuho saw us and made his way to us. He looked at Khyamyalainen with hate in his eyes and said, "You better pray to God that we are not placed in the same railroad car, for I will throw you out!"

Yuho turned to me and told me that he had shared a prison cell with Lilya's father. He said that my father-in-law had asked about me. Lilya's father did not know that I had been arrested; my father-in-law had been arrested several days before my arrest. [Urkho's father-in-law was Finnish.] According to Yuho, my father-in-law was in such poor health that he was removed and brought to the prison hospital. Nobody knows what happened to him after that. Early in the 1960s, Lilya and I received a letter stating that Peter Inki, my father-in-law, had been "rehabilitated" following his death. Later, Lilya received another letter which stated that her brother, Arvo Inki, had also been "rehabilitated" posthumously.

[The terms "rehabilitated" and "rehabilitation" in the Soviet Union referred to the political and social restoration of a person who had been repressed or criminally prosecuted without due basis. "Rehabilitation" restored the person to the state of acquittal. In many cases, "rehabilitation" was posthumous as thousands of victims had been executed or had died in prison labor camps.]

In the same crowded cell I met two of Lilya's uncles, Andrey and Joseph. [The uncles were also Finnish.] Before their arrest, they were members of a collective farm [peopled by ethnic Finns]. Andrey worked as a herdsman and Joseph was a skilled worker who could complete any task to which he was assigned. Both men were accused of belonging to an anti-Soviet rebel organization which was headed by Peter Inki, Lilya's father. The charge was a fabrication; the anti-Soviet rebel organization did not exist. My father-in-law was a village school teacher who worked with children his entire life.

We were all moved to "Kresty" prison. The prison was built during tsarist Russia and each cell was designed to hold just one or two prisoners. But due to the large number of new arrivals, the directors of the prison placed in some cells as many as nineteen prisoners. There were two beds made of iron in each cell. A primitive filthy lavatory bowl was located near the door of the cell. At night all the prisoners laid on the floor like herrings in a barrel. Even a little movement at night caused a person's neighbors to murmur. People, whose backgrounds were different from each other, were now united with the same fate—we were honest Soviet citizens who were imprisoned on false charges.

We passed the time talking to each other. Nobody knew what the future had in store. I used to speak for hours with a young man by the name of Vladimir Shtuchkov [Russian name]. We used to lie under one of the beds and discuss contemporary literature. Vladimir had begun his studies in a university but was arrested on the charge of terrorism.

Whenever a new prisoner was brought into our cell, we would ask him to tell us his profession or line of work. We would then guess the charge that had been brought against him and we would always guess right. All the students brought into the cell were accused of being "terrorists." Those who were born abroad or who had visited a foreign country, were "spies." All engineers were "saboteurs." All military men were "traitors." Those who were not ethnic Russians were accused of being "nationalists," people who were more loyal to the nation of their ethnicity than to Mother Russia.

In October a prison guard called me out of the cell: "Rukhanen, come and take along your belongings."

I was brought to another prison. It was the third prison in four months. The cells in this prison were so crowded that the men were unable to sit down. Among my fellow prisoners there was a young actor who had just graduated from an acting vocation school. He was able to recite, from the beginning to the end, [Maxim] Gorky's play entitled *On the Bottom*. The young actor had a bride but unfortunately for him, a young NKVD officer fell in love with the actor's bride and he decided to get rid of the actor. The NKVD officer discovered that the actor was born in 1916 in Teriyoki [some 30 kilometers or 18.5 miles northwest of Petrograd] in Finland. The NKVD officer used this information to accuse the actor of being a "spy."

One morning I was escorted into the main office of the prison.

"What is your patronymic name?" [A patronymic name is the name that a person inherits from his father. Jan was the first name of the father of Albert Pleysier and so the author's full name is Albert Jan Pleysier.]

"Nesterovich," I replied.

"Why is there another patronymic name in your document? You are lying! You were going to hide this from us! No tricks will save you!" After that the official used a long stream of foul words to describe me. "You will remain HERE and ROT while others will be moved out [and transported to a prison labor camp.]"

That same day almost all of the men in my cell were moved out and brought to the railway station. There were four of us who did not leave the prison cell. The authorities had found incorrectness in each of our documents [internal passports].

It was a shame that I had to stay. I wanted to leave with the others. They were being sent to a prison labor camp. I knew that it was safer for a prisoner to be brought to a labor camp as a member of a large group of prisoners than to be brought alone. I must add that not one of the prisoners with whom I became acquainted in the prison labor camp was tried in a court of law. Each was sentenced by the NKVD and by that institution alone. A prisoner's relatives who came to the prison to visit their loved one were told that he [the prisoner] had been sent to a faraway labor camp and that he would not be permitted to receive correspondence. I would never again see the men with whom I had shared a prison cell in Leningrad.

Within a short period of time the prison cell was again filled to over capacity and again it was emptied as all the prisoners except me were sent off to a prison labor camp. I continued to wait for my orders to depart. The month of October came and it went. In the middle of November I was moved back to "Kresty" and joined nine other prisoners in a cell.

I was interrogated by the young investigator who had questioned me earlier. He repeated the questions that he had asked me during my first imprisonment in "Kresty." "Tell me," he said, "about your counterrevolutionary activities." The investigator appeared tired. The interrogation was conducted without the kind of enthusiasm that he had demonstrated in the summer. The interrogation lasted only a short while and then I was escorted back to my cell.

As I lay on my wooden pallet, my thoughts turned to Lilya and my parents. I wondered why I had not received money from them for quite some time. The rules of the prison permitted relatives to send to their loved ones in prison some money every month. The directors of the prison would, in turn, give the prisoner a receipt for the amount that was sent and with that receipt the prisoner could purchase from the prison storeroom items such as cigarettes, sugar and bread. Had Lilya and my parents forgotten about me?

In January 1939, I suddenly heard a guard yell, "Rukhanen, leave and take your belongings!" As I was escorted downstairs from the fourth floor, I heard footsteps behind me. I looked back and saw Eino Salmi [Finnish name]. A guard then pushed me into a cell and moments later Eino was pushed into the same cell room.

I had met Eino in Leningrad in May 1938. At that time he told me about his arrest:

"They [the NKVD] began looking for me in June. At that time I was living in a country house near Luga and I remained there till September. When the weather turned cold, I returned to Leningrad and on the night of my return I was arrested. They [the NKVD] accused me of belonging to an anti-Soviet organization. They had already drafted a statement which identified Tobias Guttary as the leader of the organization. According to the written statement, I had expressed my doubts concerning the success of the organization. I was not sure if what the organization planned to do would succeed. Guttery had replied that Khusa and Urkho had joined the organization and with their assistance the success of the plans was guaranteed."

Eino and I did not get the opportunity to visit. The cell door opened and I heard the familiar order: "Rukhanen, let's go and take your belongings."

I must have been viewed as a dangerous criminal because they transported me alone in a "Black Raven" to the prison on Voinova Street. I was brought to a cell which held only four prisoners. For the first time during my incarceration, I had a bed all to myself. The prison had a library and prisoners were permitted to have books brought to them.

At the end of January, Lilya visited me at the prison. She had been searching for me for three months. She had spent many hours standing in long lines outside of the "Bolshoy Dom" [Big House] to get information about my whereabouts. [The Bolshoy Dom was also called the Gray House. It housed the headquarters of the NKVD in Leningrad. It was said that it consisted of nine floors above ground and that there were nine floors below the ground. The most terrible interrogations and shootings were conducted by the NKVD in the floors below the ground.] The days in prison dragged on. Much time was spent each day walking forth and back in the prison cell. One evening I added up the number of steps I had taken that day and I tried to calculate to what they were equivalent in kilometers.

I became acquainted with many men in the prisons where I was held. Each had been declared guilty of being an "enemy of the people." Yet none of the men had opposed the Soviet government and neither they nor I had ever met a genuine "enemy of the people."

The winter and spring seasons passed. Early in May, I was transported to "Kresyi" again. As I was being transported in a "Black Raven," I recollected the words of an old Finnish song: "Again I am taken for a drive from one prison to another."

In "Kresty" I shared a cell room with a young man named Lev Gumilyov. He was the son of the very famous Russian poets, Nicholas Gumilyov and Anna Akhmatova. At the time of Lev's arrest, he was studying oriental languages as a postgraduate student. He was excellent company. I taught him a Finnish song and he quickly learned to sing it like a native Finn. [Alexey Vinogradov, one of the authors of this book, knew Lev Gumilyov personally in the 1970s and 1980s. Lev was an excellent lecturer and wrote many interesting books. He died in 1992.]

On 5 December I heard the familiar: "Rukhanen, leave and take your belongings."

My cell mates congratulated me. "Now you will be released," they assured me.

When I entered the main office of the prison, one of the officers read my sentence: "The special council of the NKVD sentences Urkho Rukhanen to five years of imprisonment for his participation in an anti-Soviet nationalist organization." I had already spent seventeen months in the prisons of Leningrad and now I was to be sent to a prison labor camp. The fate of my wife, Lilya, was similar to the fate of Lev Gumilyov's mother which she described in her famous poem titled *Requiem*:

- For seventeen months I have cried

- I am calling for your return home
- I am falling down before the executioner's feet
- You are my son, you are my pain and suffering

The relatives of a prisoner were given the opportunity to visit their loved one three times during the week before his departure. Lilya was unable to visit me. She was working as a school teacher far from the city of Leningrad. My father visited me twice and Feodor, Al'ma's husband, came to visit me as well.

The visitation room within the prison was rather long and included two long latticed barriers with a corridor, one meter wide, between the latticed barriers. The prisoner who was being visited stood behind one of the latticed barriers and his visitor stood behind the other latticed barrier. Meanwhile, a prison guard walked the length of the corridor, forth and back, watching the prisoners and their visitors.

There were many visitors in the visitation room when my father arrived to see me. Everyone in the room was talking and they were all speaking quite loudly so it was difficult to hear my father. My first question was, "How are my sons doing?"

"All three are in good health."

At the time of my arrest, Lilya was pregnant with our third child and during my incarceration she gave birth to our third son. It was father who brought me the good news that Lilya and I had another son.

"What have you named him?" I asked.

"Orvo."

Father also brought me a woolen sweater and slacks that my mother had knitted. Feodor, on his visit, brought me an old sheepskin coat. These clothes would later help me survive the environment of the prison labor camp to which I was sent.

When it was time to leave I, along with other prisoners, was transported by train to the East. The carriages into which we were herded were overcrowded with men who were being sent to prison labor camps. We were not to walk around. We were only permitted to go to the washroom but were escorted by a guard. In several of the compartments in our carriage there were women. Along the way, the train would stop at the railroad stations and it would remain at each station for a long time.

At the railroad station in Sverdlovsk we were ordered to leave the cars but we were not allowed to enter the station building. [The city of Sverdlovsk was located at the geographic border between Europe and Asia.] We remained on the station platform and were ordered to squat. It was freezing outside, about 30 degrees Celsius, and there was a strong cold wind, yet we were kept in a squatted position for about an hour. Most of the prisoners had been arrested during the summer months, and they were wearing summer clothes. I was wearing the woolen clothes that father had given me and the sheepskin coat given to me by Feodor.

We were brought finally into Sverdlovsk prison and would be held there for several days. Shortly after our arrival there, a new group of prisoners from Moscow were brought into the prison. Among the new arrivals there were many former NKVD officers. Towards the end of 1938 the leadership of the NKVD was changed. [Nikolai] Yezhov was replaced by [Lavrentiy] Beriya and Beriya, in turn, replaced many of Yezhov's men with people who were loyal to him. Former leaders of the NKVD were arrested and many of them joined us as prisoners.

[On November 23, 1938, Yezhov was summoned to a meeting with Joseph Stalin, Vyacheslav Molotov and Kliment Voroshilov. It was to be Yezhov's last meeting with Stalin. At the meeting Yezhov submitted his resignation as People's Commissar of Internal Affairs. He also admitted he was guilty of letting too many "enemies of the people" get away. On the following day, the Politburo accepted Yezhov's resignation and on the 25th of November Lavrenti Beriya was appointed the new People's Commissar of Internal Affairs. As the new head of the NKVD, Beriya arrested many of Yezhov's people. By the end of 1938 as many as 332 leading NKVD executives had been arrested, 140 of them from the central apparatus and 192 from the provinces. The arrests continued into 1939 and during that year 1,364 NKVD executives were arrested.]

From Sverdlovsk we were transported to a prison labor camp in Tavda. We were housed in a large empty barrack and each of us was given a prison uniform which consisted of padded trousers, a padded jacket and an old cap. The camp was a large lumber mill with several barracks. The prisoners rolled large logs, turned the logs into wood boards and loaded the boards onto flat bed railroad cars.

At the prison labor camp, I finally received letters from Lilya and my parents. Lilya wrote that she and our sons were living in Shugozevo. [Shugozevo was a large settlement in the northeastern area of Leningrad Province.] Lilya described our sons' activities and she acquainted me with little Orvo who I had not yet seen or held. My parents wrote about themselves and what they were doing. Reading the letters was a touching and yet painful experience. I missed my family, all of them. I was a prisoner and a criminal in the eyes of the society in which my family lived. Surely, my family suffered from that reality. Lilya wrote that Reima, our oldest son, returned home from school crying. The boys at school had teased him because his father was a criminal serving time in prison.

Lilya decided to visit me at the prison labor camp in the summer of 1940. To make such a trip, a person needed money and energy. Many of Lilya's friends told her that the trip was a "crazy idea" and they tried to dissuade her from going. "Even if you should make it to Tavda," they said, "you will not be given permission to see your husband." Lilya's relatives, however, sympathized with her desire to see me and they supported her. Lilya got together food, coffee and gifts to bring to me. She purchased a train ticket and when she reached Sverdlovsk, she changed trains. After traveling another half day, she arrived in Tavda.

The director of the prison labor camp was greatly astonished when Lilya approached him to request that she be permitted to see her husband and talk to him.

"Why did you risk going on such a long difficult trip without first gaining permission to see your husband?" he asked. "We don't permit prisoners who are guilty under Article 58 to have visitors. Plus, your husband has been in the camp for only half a year."

"My husband is not guilty of the charge brought against him. That is why I have made this difficult trip, leaving my three little children in the care of my old parents."

"Everyone who is sentenced to prison claims that he is innocent but in our country no one is sent to prison unless he is guilty. If a person has been arrested by mistake, he is released. We are careful not to make a mistake," the camp director asserted.

After speaking with the camp director for a long time, Lilya was given permission to meet with me for one hour but under the supervision of a camp guard. That evening, after I returned from work, I was called to the office room used by the camp guards. Lilya rushed to embrace me; she kissed me many times, once for each of our sons, once for my mother and once for my father. The kissing would continue for quite some time until the camp guard lost his patience and yelled: "Stop licking!" He told us where to sit and warned that we were to speak Russian only. It had been two long years since my arrest and there was so much that we wanted to share. We tried to speak in Russian but inevitably we would use our native language, Finnish. The camp guard warned us that he would immediately end our meeting if he heard us use another word of our "wild language."

The hour went by as if it was a minute. The camp guard looked at his watch and we knew it was over. We became terribly sad. Tears fell from Lilya's eyes. I tried to comfort Lilya but I too was weeping. I suggested that she go to the town of Irbit which was the location of the management office of the Northern Ural Prison Labor Camps. I told Lilya that it might be possible to receive permission for us to spend some time together privately in a room without the supervision of a camp guard.

Lilya went to see the foreman of the wood processing factory where I worked. He told Lilya that I was a member of his best work crew. He advised Lilya to see the supervisor of the prison camp and ask him to write a review of her husband's work and behavior and then to bring the supervisor's comments to Irbit with a request to spend some private time with her husband.

Lilya did that. The supervisor wrote down what he thought of my work and behavior and promised to send his comments to Irbit. (see Map)

Lilya traveled by train to Irbit, a trip that took seven hours. She found the main office of the Northern Ural Prison Labor Camps and asked to see the chief director of management. She was not granted permission to see him. Lilya went back the next day and repeated her request, but again the people in the office would not permit her to see the chief director. Lilya did not give up; she stayed in Irbit and tried several more times to get an audience with the chief director.

Then one day Lilya met, in the hotel where she was staying, a director of one of the departments of the Northern Ural Prison Labor Camps. He and his wife sympathized with Lilya. It was with their assistance that Lilya was admitted into the building that housed the main office of the people who managed the Northern Ural Prison Labor Camps. She checked in her coat at the cloak room and then left the building to go to a beauty salon to get her hair styled, her fingernails painted and her lips and eyelids colored. She then returned and made her way to the upper floor where the chief director had his office. Lilya saw a long line of people, all waiting to see the chief director. She decided not to stand in line but walked through the chief director's office door as soon as someone exited the office. She told the people standing in line, as she walked past them, that her presence had been requested and it was urgent that she see the chief director. The people in line assumed that Lilya was a member of the chief director's staff.

The chief director looked surprised as Lilya walked into his office.

"Who are you and what do you want?" he asked.

"It concerns a personal matter."

"Well since you are here, please sit down and tell me about your problem."

"I came to ask for your permission to have some private time with my husband who is a prisoner in a prison labor camp in Tavda. The supervisor of the camp has sent you his opinion of my husband."

The chief director asked his secretary to bring him the supervisor's letter and after reading the supervisor's comments he told Lilya:

"Your husband has been in the prison camp only six months. The private meeting you are requesting is awarded to prisoners who have earned it by working hard and demonstrating a behavior that is excellent. Such an award is not given to those who have been at the prison camp for only a half of a year."

"I am a mother of three children, I am a school teacher, and I have spent my entire vacation traveling thousands of kilometers to come here to see my husband. I do not know if I will be able to continue doing my job if I am not permitted to be with my husband before leaving Tavda."

"It is hard to believe, as attractive as you are, that you find it necessary to be with your husband," the chief director responded.

"You are greatly mistaken!" Lilya retorted.

The chief director drummed the desk with his fingers for a while, then called his secretary into the office and ordered her to type a permission form granting Lilya a private meeting with her husband for two hours.

With this permission form, Lilya returned to Tavda. She showed the form to the supervisor of the prison labor camp and requested, as her new friends in Irbit had advised, that the two hours be divided into two parts.

That evening, after all the prisoners had gone to bed, Lilya and I were brought to a special room where we were able to spend time together. We spent the entire night together. The next evening we met again and again we spent the entire night together.

The winter months of 1940/41 proved to be the most difficult for me during my residence at the prison labor camp. It was freezing cold. I was one of a large group of prisoners that was marched to Karabashskiy, some 30 kilometers [18.5 miles] from our camp. It was a new site. There were no barracks at the site, so we slept in tents. After eating our portions of soup, we fell asleep in our clothes. Fortunately, I was able to secure for myself a top bed. The top beds were warmer than the lower beds.

We were awakened at 6:00 in the morning and then we ran to the forest to get our portions of bread and soup. After breakfast, we were assigned the tools that we were to use to cut down trees. I was handed a whip saw. I had never used such a tool. We were also given instructions on how to cut down trees. We were told where to stand when cutting a tree and how to handle the saw. We were instructed not to leave a tall stump. But we had never cut down trees in high snow and the stumps that we left, were too tall. So we were forced to cut the tree stumps again but this time the cuts were to be closer to the ground.

All that winter we sawed down trees—pines and birches. As spring approached, we pulled the large tree trunks, using horses, to the shore of a nearby river. However, the river, that spring, did not rise and it could not be used to transport the trees. The trees were left to rot by the riverside and all of our hard work went to waste.

Working in the snow, cutting down trees, in freezing temperatures was difficult. There were many men who found the work too difficult. I remember Nicholas Zouzelkov who had worked in Leningrad as an artist [painter]. He had difficulty removing the branches from the fallen trees. The supervisor noticed this and walked up to him criticizing him saying:

"What kind of a man are you that you can't do a simple job as this?" Zouzelkov replied, "But I can play the piano. Can you do that?"

Throughout my entire imprisonment at the prison labor camp, I worked as a lumberman. Everyday, before sunrise, we made our way to the forest, a distance of 8 kilometers (5 miles) away. If they wanted us to work at a new section of the forest, a supervisor would accompany us and with an axe would mark the borders of our work area. We were not to go outside of the marked area. The person who was caught outside of the area, could expect to be shot on the spot. During the winter months, no one was tempted to leave the work zone. But during the summer, the mushrooms and berries that grew outside of the work zone became a temptation for some of the men. Once, in 1942, a prison guard shot a prisoner in the leg for being outside of the work zone. The prisoner had tried to get a mushroom just 5 meters [16 feet] outside of the work zone.

Cutting down trees is difficult in freezing temperatures especially if you are constantly hungry. We were ordered to cut down only healthy birch trees which were to be used to make veneer. We would not get credit for cutting down an unhealthy birch. If that should happen, we would not receive our normal portion of daily bread.

The presence of lice was a great irritation. The lice lived around my neck under the collar of my coat. I was unable to scratch my neck because I carried my saw and axe on my shoulders and I wore heavy mittens to protect my hands from the cold. I would often remember the Finnish proverb: "When the lice are biting, all mankind hates you." Every evening we would shake the lice from our clothes above the burning hot "burzhuika" and watch the lice jump and hear them crackle like fireworks. [A burzhuika is a metal enclosed stove that is fueled with wood. The heat generated by the stove burned the lice.]

We wore bast sandals. [It is footwear made with the bark of birch trees.] The sandals wore well during dry weather. During the winter we would wear galoshes over the sandals and our feet remained quite warm. But if the ground was wet, the sandals would come apart. One spring we had to cross a marsh. The snow under our feet was as soft as sponge but underneath the wet snow there was a layer of solid ice. Consequently, my sandals came apart when they became saturated with water so I was forced to walk the last several kilometers barefooted. Even the camp guard who was with us was moved to pity by the pain that I suffered. Both of my feet became inflamed and I would suffer from phlegmon for a long time. It was an illness that scarred my feet. Years later, while I was bathing in a communal bath house, a little boy noticed my feet and asked if I had been wounded in a war.

At the camp we would talk about a variety of subjects but the most common topic was our imprisonment. Why had we been arrested? What was the significance of our arrest and imprisonment? Many of us knew we were being exploited but no one could voice the reason or reasons why. "I know why you are here," a prisoner once said to me, "because you are a Finn, but I don't know the reason for my being here."

June 26, 1943, was the last day of my five year sentence. At the end of June, I was called to the office of the supervisor of the prison labor camp. I could feel my heart beating with excitement as I made my way to the office: "Is it possible," I asked myself, "that the end of my suffering is finally here?"

When I entered the office, the supervisor told me that he had received orders to postpone my release until further notice. "Oh, Perkele," the words came involuntarily from my lips. "Why was my release being postponed?" I asked myself. "Is it possible that they plan never to release me? Why not? They can do whatever they want." All hope that I would ever be released suddenly vanished. [Perkele is translated Devil and is used by Finns as a curse word.]

The remainder of 1943 passed and the year 1944 came and went. We worked hard. The war against Germany came to an end. I received a telegram from Lilya and my sons. In it they expressed their congratulations with the nation's victory and hoped that, with the war now over, I would soon be given my freedom.

The long awaited freedom did not come. The Soviet Union went to war against Japan and I was forced to remain working at the prison labor camp. But I was not the only one at the camp whose discharge was postponed. We discussed it among ourselves and concluded that our discharge was being postponed due to the war against Japan.

In September 1945, the war against Japan came to an end. But we were still not discharged. We were forced to work another winter season in the frozen forest. Many of us lost all hope that we would be released.

In August 1946, one of the camp guards approached me with good news. "Rukhanen," he said, "hurry, finish your daily quota because I have good news." That was his way of informing me that I was to be released. Nevertheless, I was still required to complete my quota of work for that day.

A Hungarian by the name of Haier and I were released from the prison labor camp on the same day. Before we left, we were given some food, just enough to sustain us as we made our way to Tavda where the management office of the Northern Ural Prison Labor Camps was located. [The management office had been moved from Irbit to Tavda.] Haier and I left the prison camp at 3 in the morning. We had ahead of us a 12 kilometer [7.5 mile] walk to a landing pier where a tugboat was to take us to Tavda. It was a walk in the dark and we walked through forests and fields. The high grass was covered with dew and when we reached the landing pier we were wet from our feet to our waist. We waited all day for the tugboat, but it never arrived. In the evening we were told about a truck that was going to Tavda and the driver gave us a ride.

It was dark when we arrived in Tavda. We didn't know anyone in Tavda and we knew that no one in the community would give shelter to former prisoners. We found a prison labor camp and asked one of the guards if we could sleep in the camp. He turned us away and directed us to a nearby horse barn. In the barn we each found an empty stall and that night we slept on the hay in our stalls.

It took the people at the office of management several days to prepare our documents. During that time, we continued living in the horse barn. Finally, I was given a passport that was valid for one year. [It was an internal passport which was used by the State to control and monitor the internal movement and residence of a citizen. The passport recorded the following information: sex, surname, first name and patronymic, date and place of birth, ethnicity, family status and record of military service.] I was also given some food and money for a railway ticket. The train was to take me east to Krasnoyarskiy Province where Lilya and my sons were living at that time. Haier went west.[1]

NOTE

1. Урхо Руханен, В вихрях века [In Whirlwinds of the Century] (Петрозаводск, Карелия, 1987), Стр. 81–106.

Chapter Three

Stalin's Campaign against Cosmopolitanism and Zionism

The Great Patriotic War (1941–1945), brought to the Soviet Union enormous losses in human lives and materials. During the war, hundreds of thousands of Soviet citizens had gone to the West, either as forced labor or of their own will and many never returned to their homeland. Large numbers of Red Army soldiers died on the battlefields as well as in the prison camps administered by the enemy, the Germans. Whole categories of people such as Soviet Jews and Gypsies, Communist Party members and Soviet government officials were exterminated by the Germans wherever they were found. Soviet partisan warfare against the enemy led to reprisals against the civilian populations and many Soviet citizens were executed. It has been estimated that more than twenty million Soviet citizens lost their lives and that the losses were evenly divided between military personnel and civilians.

The material losses were also huge. In addition to the destruction suffered during the fighting, large areas of the Soviet Union were devastated at the hands of the retreating Red Army in 1941. The Soviet forces carried out a scorched-earth policy, trying to destroy anything that might be of value to the invading enemy. When the Germans were forced to abandon Soviet territory, in 1944, they tried as they withdrew to destroy anything that might be of value to the advancing Red Army. They flooded and wrecked mines and blew up bridges and railroad tracks. Much of Soviet Russia became a wasteland. According to official figures, Soviet material losses included the partial or total destruction of as many as 1,700 towns, 70,000 villages, 84,000 schools, 43 libraries, 31,000 factories and 1,300 bridges. The Soviet economy lost some 137,000 tractors and 49,000 combine harvesters as well as 7,000,000 horses, 17,000,000 cows, 20,000,000 pigs and 27,000,000 sheep and goats.[1]

To repair the damage that was done by the war and to reestablish economic advance, Joseph Stalin initiated the Fourth Five-Year Plan which was begun in 1946. The plan placed great emphasis on the development of heavy industries, particularly the production of coal, electric power, iron, steel, timber, cement, agricultural machinery and lorries (trucks). Russian industries, especially heavy industries, were supposed to achieve new heights in production, while labor productivity was to rise significantly. Every effort was to be made to get the Soviet people to work hard and long hours. The Fourth Five-Year Plan also called for the construction of military goods. Stalin believed that the Soviet Union needed to prepare for a war against the capitalistic powers in the West.

To rebuild and expand agriculture, Stalin's government completed the collectivization program which had been started in 1928. Small collective farms were incorporated into large agricultural complexes. The ultimate goal was to convert the Soviet peasants into members of a rural proletariat, working in what might be identified as "farm factories." But the effort at transforming the agricultural population into good socialists was met with considerable discontent. As a consequence, the agricultural outputs in the latter 1940s were far below the prewar levels.

The Fourth Five-Year Plan did not emphasize the needs or comforts of the Soviet citizens. Despite the government's promise of a better life to come after the war, the standard of living for most Soviet citizens did not improve. In fact, nothing much had changed since the 1930s which was a decade of sacrifice and austerity. The low standard of living to which most citizens were subjected was very evident to the Red Army soldiers who returned home after defeating Germany and its allies. During the war, as the Red Army drove the enemy back to Germany, the Soviet soldiers noticed that the industrial workers and farmers of Eastern Europe enjoyed a much higher standard of living than the Soviet citizens. For years, the Soviet people had been told by their government that life in the Soviet Union was much better than life for their counterparts in the West. It was a lie and the returning Soviet soldiers realized it was a lie.

Peter Gornev was a Red Army officer and a member of the Communist Party who believed less and less in Stalin's regime and "its promises." When he and his soldiers occupied the eastern half of Poland following the Soviet Union's invasion of that country in September of 1939, he was shocked by the high standard of living enjoyed by Poland's workers. Peter expressed his initial impressions of Poland in the following paragraphs:

"At 5:00 A.M., September 17, 1939, the Red Army crossed the Polish border. We moved ahead almost without resistance. Could Poland possibly resist Germany and the USSR at the same time?

"By the twenty first, the Red Army had occupied all previously agreed upon areas. This was not war. It was a poorly organized triumphal march. In

Poland, all of us, officers and men, saw the riches and prosperity of a capitalist country and couldn't believe our eyes. We had never believed there could be such abundance of goods and at such low prices—especially not in 'backward' Poland. Our [Soviet] propaganda had described her [Poland] as a backward nation.

"Upon entering a town, our troops descended upon the stores and bought up everything in sight, particularly dress material. The buying spree was understandable, but the local population couldn't figure it out.

"'Tell me sir,' a Polish salesman once asked, 'why do your men buy all sorts of trash, not even bothering to ask the price? If you tell me that you don't have such things I couldn't believe it. You have such big tanks and so many of them!'

"I did not answer the query.

"This first meeting with the capitalist world had come too unexpectedly and was too stunning. It gave many of us a shock and directed us toward new thoughts and understanding. Those who had at first honestly believed we were going to free our class brothers, found themselves overcome by doubt.

"'Comrade Colonel,' I was asked by my chauffeur, 'didn't we come to Poland to liberate our brothers, oppressed by landowners and capitalists? We have traveled far together. We have been in towns and villages, but I have seen no class brothers of mine. To me they all look like kulaks and bourgeois. A peasant has three or four horses, five or six cows; there is a bicycle in front of every house. Workers wear suits, hats—the same as a big Soviet director. There is something here that I don't understand.'"[2]

The prosperity witnessed by Gornev and his chauffeur in Poland in 1939 and the influences to which the Soviet soldiers were exposed as they drove the Germans back through Eastern Europe in 1944 and into Berlin in 1945, concerned Stalin. He was a student of history and was very familiar with the Decembrist Revolt which had taken place in St. Petersburg, Russia more than a century before. Thus, just a few days after the Soviet forces established their control over Berlin, Stalin told Konstantin Simonov, a well known Soviet writer, that he did not want a repeat of what had happened after Russia's victory over Napoleon I in 1814. "Stalin feared a new Decembrist movement," Simonov wrote. "He felt that he had introduced Ivan [the Russian soldiers] to Europe and Europe to Ivan. [This is] . . . what [Tsar] Alexander I had done in 1813–14 . . ."[3] (see Glossary—Simonov, Konstantin)

Stalin knew that the Russian officers fighting for Tsar Alexander I had been impressed by the personal liberties and the economic prosperity that they encountered during their occupation of Paris following Napoleon's surrender. What they witnessed in Paris inspired them to fight for political and social changes in Russia after they returned to their homeland. Their efforts culminated about a decade later in St. Petersburg, Russia's capital city.

On December 14, 1825, military officers commanding almost 3,000 men stationed in St. Petersburg led their soldiers to Senate Square and had them stand in formation around the equestrian statue of Peter the Great. It marked the beginning of what became known as the Decembrist Revolt. Earlier, the officers and their soldiers had refused to swear allegiance to the newly crowned Tsar Nicholas I and had instead proclaimed their loyalty to the idea of a Russian constitution. The men in the square expected to be joined by many more rebel soldiers but they never arrived. The plan was to seize the Winter Palace and arrest the newly crowned tsar and his family. A constitution would then be drafted and during the interim period the country would be ruled by a dictator, who had already been chosen. The dictator would rule for a few days or weeks and his place would be taken by a provisional government. The provisional government would, in turn, be replaced by a Grand Assembly, a representative body elected by the people of Russia.

The Decembrist Revolt ended in failure. The chosen dictator, Prince Sergei Trubetskoy (a military officer who had distinguished himself against Napoleon's forces in battles fought at Borodino, Maloyavoslavets and Leipsig) never arrived at Senate Square. Earlier in the day (December 14) he panicked and decided not to lead the revolt. With the defection of Prince Trubetskoy, the rebel soldiers were left leaderless.

Tsar Nicholas I responded to the revolt by sending emissaries to the rebel soldiers urging them to leave Senate Square and return to their barracks. They refused. The tsar then assembled on Senate Square and in the streets leading up to the square some 12,000 soldiers who were loyal to the tsar. As the day turned dark, the tsar ordered his artillery brigades to open fire on the rebel soldiers. Within ten minutes the rebel soldiers fled and most of those who survived the skirmish were arrested and marched to prison. Prince Trubetskoy was arrested as well and sent east to work in the coal mines of Nevchinst. Kondraty Ryleyev, another important Decembrist leader (as a military officer he had fought against Napoleon's armies in Poland, Prussia and France) was arrested and hanged.

Stalin was determined to avoid an uprising similar to the Decembrist Revolt. The soldiers of the Red Army who occupied Berlin following Germany's surrender had come into contact with British and American soldiers. They had become familiar with Western ways of doing things and with Western freedoms. They had purchased Western consumer items such as cigarette lighters and wristwatches. According to Stalin, they had been infected with the dangerous Western values that he had tried to expunge from Soviet society before the war and that he would try to keep out of the Soviet Union after the war. To some degree, the returning Soviet veterans were perceived as a threat by Stalin. Thus, the formation of veterans' groups was prohibited. Veterans were also discouraged from expressing their opinions in public and from writing their memoirs.

In 1946 Stalin initiated a campaign against any and all attitudes that he considered harmful to Soviet values. The campaign was entrusted to Andrei Zhdanov, a Politburo member and the Commissar for Culture. The campaign, which was later named Zhdanovshchina (Zhdanov's reign), consisted of measures that were designed to purge anti-Soviet elements and decadent Western influences from literature, art and music. The fine arts, it was decided, must serve the purposes of Marxism, Leninism and Stalinism, and should be so crafted that they would instill within Soviet citizens national patriotism.

The starting point of the campaign was the city of Leningrad when on August 14, 1946, the Central Committee of the Communist Party issued a decree censoring two literary journals, *Zvezda* (The Star) and *Leningrad,* for publishing the "debased" works of two Leningrad writers, Mikhail Zoshchenko and Anna Akhmatova. Zoshchenko was a satirist and Stalin had long been irritated by his stories. Especially annoying was Zoshchenko's *Adventures of a Monkey* published in 1946. It was a satire about a monkey who escaped from a zoo during the war.

Zhdanov denounced the short story with the following comments:

"If you will read that story carefully and think it over, you will see that Zoshchenko casts the monkey in the role of the supreme judge of our social order. . . . The monkey is presented as a kind of rational principle having the right to evaluate the conduct of human beings. The picture of Soviet life is deliberately and vilely distorted, and caricatured so that Zoshchenko can put into the mouth of his monkey the vile, poisonous anti-Soviet sentiment to the effect that life is better in the zoo than at liberty and that one breathes more easily in a cage than among Soviet people. Is it possible to sink to a lower political and moral level? And how could the Leningraders endure to publish in their journals such fifth and nonsense?"[4]

Zoshchenko's work, Zhdanov concluded, was "a vile obscenity." It violated the doctrine of Socialist Realism which demanded that the various forms of fine art, such as literature, must depict some aspect of the human struggle toward socialist progress for a better life. According the Zhdanov, the outstanding heroes of literary works are those who portray "real" life and whose main characters are optimistic and heroic. At the same time their written works educate the masses in socialism.

The official denunciation of Zoshchenko was quickly translated into action. Zoshchenko was expelled from the Union of Soviet Writers. (see Glossary—Union of Soviet Writers) Barred from publication, Zoshchenko was forced to work as a translator and resume his first career as a shoemaker. Following Stalin's death in 1953, he was readmitted to the Union of Soviet Writers. But by this time, Zoshchenko had fallen into such a deep depression that he produced no major writings before his death in 1958. Anna Akhmatova like Zoshchenko did not promote Socialist Realism. She was a distinguished Russian poet whose main themes were love and religion. Zhdanov denounced her, claiming that her poetry was "empty, inane, and alien to our people. . . . Her verse, nourished in the spirit of pessimism and decadence . . . cannot be tolerated in Soviet literature." Zhdanov wrote: "[Her] subject matter is throughout individualist. The range of her poetry is pathetically limited. It is the poetry of a half-crazy gentile lady, who tosses back and forth between the bedroom and the chapel. . . . Half-nun and half harlot, or rather both nun and harlot, her harlotry is mingled with prayer."[5]

Akhmatova, like Zoshchenko, was removed from Union of Soviet Writers. She was forced to remain silent, living isolated and poor until she could publish again after Stalin's death. A two-volume edition of Akhmatova's collected works was published in Moscow in 1986 and *The Complete Poems of Anna Akhmatova*, also in two volumes, appeared in 1990.

The attacks against Zoshchenko and Akhmatova were followed by a series of repressive measures against "cosmopolitanism" in the fine arts and sciences. (The word "cosmopolitan" is derived from two Greek words, "kosmos" meaning "world" and "polites" meaning "citizen." In its etymology, therefore, a "cosmopolitan" is a citizen of the world, rather than a citizen of a particular country.) One of Russia's early cosmopolitans was Alexander Veselovsky (1838–1906), a historian of literature and a literary theorist. He maintained that literature is the product of influences that originate worldwide and not in just one country. He came to this conclusion while he was studying medieval Italian literature. He discovered that many literary devices were exported to Europe from the Orient through Byzantium. In 1947, the ideas of Veselovsky were attacked because they were "cosmopolitan." Under Zhdanovshchina, "cosmopolitanism" became a term of abuse. Whereas once it had been praiseworthy to be called a citizen of the world, the term "cosmopolitan" was now identified with "servility to the West."

The anti-cosmopolitan campaign intensified in 1948 and reached its zenith on January 28, 1949. On this day *Pravda* published an article in which several theater critics were criticized for not fully appreciating State approved plays that were designed to educate and elevate the peoples' consciousness. (see Glossary—Pravda) "At a time," the article complained, "when we are faced with acute problems and standing against rootless 'cosmopolitanism,' against manifestations of bourgeois influences alien to the people, these critics do not find anything better to do than to discredit the most progressive events in our literature."[6] All the critics were expelled eventually from the Communist Party and from the Union of Soviet Writers.

Anti-cosmopolitanism led to a widespread purge of educators and writers. Educators who encouraged their students to read and study the works of foreign scholars and writers were accused of "cosmopolitanism." It was believed that they were exposing the students to ideas that might cause their young minds to question the values of the Soviet system. Soviet writers who had mentioned the Western influences on Russia's great writers of the past were denounced. Since Maxim Gorky (Alexei M. Peshkov, 1869–1936) was already dead (he had been one of Stalin's favorite writers), he escaped denunciation for acknowledging the debt that he owed to certain Western writers. Although the anti-cosmopolitan campaign did not lead to mass executions, people were arrested and tortured. Mostly, the State used administrative measures to discipline or punish those who were charged with promoting "cosmopolitanism." The State also sealed off foreign contacts and influences. In the end, the anti-cosmopolitan campaign succeeded in getting the intellectual establishment to support strongly Soviet Communism.

Everything Russian was to be glorified and the achievements of the West were to be minimized. Failure to do so as a historian was dangerous. Even Anna Pankvatova, one of the leading Soviet historians and a person loyal to the ideas of Marxism-Leninism, was scolded for voicing the importance of the Western philosophers. Pankvatova had made the mistake of acknowledging the influence that the writings of philosophers such as Jean Rousseau had on Alexander Radishchev (1749–1802). Rousseau had championed personal liberties. At the time that Pankvatova made her comments, Radishchev was being portrayed by Soviet historians as one of the early Russian revolutionaries who believed that revolution was the sole means to a better social order.

In 1790 Radishchev published his book *Journey from Petersburg to Moscow* in which he described the horrors of serfdom. While en route from St. Petersburg to Moscow, Radishchev witnessed serfs working on a Sunday, because only on that day could they work on their own land; the rest of the week was devoted to the landlords whose property they were. Radishchev witnessed, at an auction, the sale of the members of a single serf family to different buyers. "Oh," Radishchev wrote, "would that the slaves [serfs] burdened with heavy shackles should rise in their despair and with the irons that deprive them of freedom crush our heads!" (Radishchev was the son of a well-to-do landowner.) Radishchev called for an end to autocracy and despotism and suggested that Russia become a republic and that every individual be given full liberties. When Catherine the Great was informed about Radishchev's book, she had him arrested calling him "a rebel worse than [Yemelian] Pugachev." Radishchev was interrogated and sentenced to death. Catherine commuted the sentence and exiled Radishchev to Siberia.

In 1948, the campaign against "cosmopolitanism" adopted anti-Zionism. Despite Stalin's anti-Semitism, he had been an early supporter of a Jewish nation in Palestine. He hoped to turn it into a Soviet satellite state in the Middle East. When the Jewish nation of Israel, established in 1948, turned to the United States for aid and support, Stalin became concerned about the pro-Israeli feeling harbored by the Soviet Jews. (There lived in the Soviet Union some two million people identified as Jews.) Stalin suspected the Soviet Jews of becoming a fifth column for the United States of America (The Soviet

Union was at war with the United States of America, the Cold War.) His concerns were reinforced by Golda Myerson (later Meir). She arrived in Moscow in the autumn of 1948 as the first Israeli ambassador to the Soviet Union. Everywhere she went, she was cheered by crowds of Soviet Jews.

Anyone who openly favored the new nation of Israel or applauded the accomplishments of Jewish intellectuals, came under suspicion. When the renowned Soviet author Konstantin Simonov was accused of keeping the wrong company, it was in reference to his association with Soviet Jewish writers. Simonov responded with a scathing speech to a meeting of playwrights and critics in Moscow. Part of the speech was printed in *Pravda* on February 28, 1949:

> "The harmful activity of cosmopolitanism cannot be reduced only to the spheres of art and science, but it also has political implications. The propaganda of bourgeois cosmopolitanism now aids the world reactionaries and those who want a new war. Cosmopolitanism is the imperialists' policy and at the same time it seeks to weaken patriotism and afterwards to deliver the people to the American monopolies. Cosmopolitanism in art aims to deprive people of pride in their national roots and to run down their national pride, at which point they can be sold as slaves to American imperialism."[7]

Stalin was pleased with Simonov's anti-cosmopolitan stance and in 1950, as a reward, placed the writer in charge of one of the Soviet Union's top literary newspapers, the *Literary Gazette*. (see Glossary—Union of Soviet Writers) As the paper's chief editor, Simonov dismissed all of the paper's Jewish writers for their "poor work and political mistakes." Some of those who were dismissed were friends of Simonov. (see Glossary—Simonov, Konstantin)

In late 1952 Stalin was provoked to begin planning a great purge against the Soviet Jews. The provocation was the so-called "doctors' plot" (physicians' plot). The affair came about at the initiative of ranking officials within the Ministry of State Security who were aware of Stalin's anti-Semitism. Among those arrested were prominent Kremlin physicians whose patients were Stalin and other top Party and State officials as well as top army officers. The physicians were accused with planning to undermine the health of the leadership of the Soviet Union. Of the nine physicians who were accused, seven were Jews. As a pretext, an accusation was drafted by Lidiya Timashuk, a radiologist at the Kremlin hospital. Under horrible tortures, the accused physicians confessed to having taken part in a plot to murder Party, government and army leaders through the conscious use of incorrect medical treatment.

The story of the "doctors' plot" was published by *Pravda* on January 13, 1953. The article was headlined: "Vicious Spies and Killers under the Mask of Academic Physicians." The article mentioned the names of most of the physicians and noted that the "terrorist group" had ties to an "international Jewish bourgeois" organization that was guided by American intelligence services. The following excerpts are taken from the article in *Pravda*:

> "Today the TASS [Telegraph Agency of the Soviet Union] news agency reported the arrest of a group of saboteur-doctors. This terrorist group, uncovered some time ago by organs of state security, had as their goal shortening the lives of the leaders of the Soviet Union by means of medical sabotage.
>
> "Among the victims of this band of inhuman beasts were Comrades A.A. Zhdanov and A.S. Shcherbakov. [Andrei Zhdanov died suddenly in August 1948.] The criminals confessed that taking advantage of the illness of Comrade Zhdanov, they intentionally concealed a minor cardial infection, prescribed inadvisable treatments for this serious illness and thus killed Comrade Zhdanov.
>
> "The majority of the participants of the terrorist group - Vorsi, B. Kogan, Feldman, Grinshtein, Etinger and others—were bought by American intelligence. They were recruited by a branch-office of American intelligence—the international Jewish bourgeois—nationalist organization called 'Joint.' [Joint apparently referred to the American Jewish Joint Distribution Committee, a philanthropic organization of American Jews for overseas aid.] The filthy face of this Zionist spy organization, covering up their vicious actions under the mask of kindness, is now completely revealed.
>
> "Unmasking the gang of poisoner-physicians struck a blow against the international Jewish Zionist organization. Now all can see what sort of philanthropists and 'friends of peace' hid beneath the sign-board of 'Joint.'
>
> "All this is true, of course. But it is also true, apart from these enemies, we still have another enemy: the lack of vigilance of our people. One may not doubt that, as long as we are absent-minded, there will be sabotage. Consequently, in order to liquidate sabotage, it is necessary to purge lack of vigilance from our ranks."[8]

Scientists, writers and other figures from the Soviet cultural world denounced the "physician-murderers." The *Literary Gazette*, whose chief editor was Konstantin Simonov, published a vicious article entitled "Murderers in White Coats." At the Party meeting in the Presidium of the United Soviet Socialist Republics Academy of Sciences, respectable academicians demanded the death penalty for the physicians. Meetings were organized all over the Soviet Union and those in attendance expressed their outrage and denounced the "physician-murderers." Patients refused to accept treatment from Jewish physicians, maintaining that they would be poisoned. Many Jewish physicians were driven out of clinics and hospitals. Jews were insulted, attacked and even beaten. Lidiya Timashuk, for her vigilance and for reporting the "physician-murderers," was awarded the Order of Lenin. (see Glossary—Order of Lenin)

Stalin was personally in charge of the "doctors' plot." His scenario was divided into several stages. First, the physicians were to be made to confess to the charges brought against them. Next, the victims were to be hanged in Red Square in Moscow. The public executions were then to be followed by pogroms throughout the Soviet Union. The pogroms would cause Jewish personalities from the world of culture to turn to Stalin requesting that he protect the Soviet Jews by giving them permission to leave the cities and return to the land. Finally, there would be a mass deportation of Jews, "at their own request," to the eastern territories of the Soviet Union. The request, which was to be made by the leading Soviet Jews, was already written and had already been signed. If Stalin's anti-Zionist purge had been implemented, it would have resulted in a wave of terror against Jews throughout the Soviet Union.

The purge did not occur because on March 5, 1953, Stalin died. He suffered a cerebral hemorrhage with a loss of consciousness and paralysis of the right arm and leg. Although it is generally accepted that Soviet citizens at large grieved Stalin's death, in the prison labor camps the responses to his passing varied. Some prisoners wanted to donate money for a memorial wreath. Others accepted the news of his death "in tomb-like silence." Many prisoners and guards were confused; they did not know what to expect now that Stalin was gone.

One of the prisoners was a Jewish lady by the name of Sofia Prupis. In the latter 1940s, four of her professors at Leningrad State University were arrested and interrogated by the MGB. (See Glossary—Soviet secret police) Each was declared guilty of the charges that were brought against them and one of the charges was "cosmopolitanism."

In 1949, Sofia was also arrested by the MGB. She was charged with being a Trotskyite and a Zionist. (See the Appendix, Leon Trotsky and Trotskyism and Political Zionism.) Sofia was declared guilty of treason and given a ten-year prison sentence under Article 58 paragraph 10 within the Criminal Code of the Russian Soviet Federated Socialist Republic. She was exiled to a prison labor camp located in a northern region of the Soviet Union. In 1998, Sofia shared with the authors of the book her life story from the days when she was a child up to the time when she returned to Leningrad following her release from the prison labor camp where she served her prison sentence. The following chapters are a record of Sofia's recollections.

NOTES

1. Nicholas V. Riasanovsky, A History of Russia (London: Oxford University Press, 1969), 585.

2. Louis Fischer, Thirteen Who Fled (New York: Harper and Brothers, 1949), 36–37.
3. Martin Sixsmith, Russia: A 1,000-Year Chronicle of the Wild East (New York: The Overlook Press, 2014), 366.
4. Edward J. Brown, Russian Literature since the Revolution (Cambridge, Massachusetts: Harvard University Press, 1982), 226-–27.
5. Brown, Russian Literature since the Revolution, 227.
6. Pravda, January 28, 1949.
7. Pravda, February 28, 1949.
8. Pravda, January 13, 1953.

Chapter Four

Sofia's Early Life

I was born into a Jewish family on December 28, 1919, in the Surazhsk District of the Vitebsk Province of Belorussia. Yanovichi was the name of our village. My family had moved to Yanovichi from Lithuania before I was born. Prupis, my maiden name, is Lithuanian. I don't know why and when the family left Lithuania, but I do know that my grandparents lived in Belorussia and that they had relatives in Lithuania. My grandmother died when I was little. Grandfather, Joseph, was an old man.

Our family consisted of five people. My father, Mendel, bought and sold cattle. My mother, Musa Berkovna, was a beautiful woman and a good housekeeper. She worked hard on the farm and in our kitchen garden. She had golden hands, turning that which was worthless into something that was valuable. I was the oldest of the three children. My brother Pavel was born in 1921 and my sister Anna was born in 1925.

I remember the night that mother gave birth to Anna. I was sleeping in the children's bedroom and was awakened by a scream. I opened my eyes and saw a woman with basins running forth and back in the living room. I saw father sitting at the table, praying. When he noticed that I was awake, he invited me into my parents' bedroom to see my newly born sister. After a while, I was disappointed in having a sister because it was my duty to take care of her and to take her for walks as she lay in the baby carriage.

My father was a true believer. He told me that his grandparents and great grandparents were Jewish priests. I believe it was my father who instilled within me the importance of truthfulness, the conviction that I must always be honest. I believe that religion, both the Judaic faith and Russian Orthodoxy, established and maintained good moral principles within Russian society before the Bolsheviks came to power. I further believe that the moral basis of a person's character is established during the early years of the person's life and within a family setting.

We owned a rather large farm. Our house had an enclosed porch which included a large storage area. It had a wide kitchen with a stove. The other rooms included my parents' bedroom, grandfather's room, the children's bedroom, a very small wash room and the family living room. Our kitchen garden was behind the house. In it we grew potatoes, carrots, beets, beans, cabbages, cucumbers and other vegetables. In the backyard we also had a variety of fruit trees; we had apple trees, plum trees and pear trees. There was a large barn in the backyard where we kept several cows, two horses and many chickens.

We never suffered from hunger. For breakfast we usually had gruel or milk with bread. For lunch we had a vegetable or cereal soup [shchi, borsch or something similar] and potatoes or gruel. For supper we ate potatoes with salted cabbage or cucumbers. We also ate bread and had curds, cream and milk. Our meals were typical for "middle income" peasants. On holidays mother would prepare especially delicious food. As Jews we ate kosher meat and other kosher foods. A fried goose was always on our table on Easter and during the other holidays.

Mother's brother, Uncle Arkadiy, attended the Leningrad Technological University and earned a degree in electrical engineering. Following his graduation in 1924 or 1925, he and his wife were sent to a newly constructed electric power station near the city of Chelyabinsk. Uncle Arkadiy and his wife had no children.

When Uncle Arkadiy learned that it was becoming more and more difficult for us to live in Belorussia, he urged my parents to come and move to Chelyabinsk. My parents agreed that it was wise to move and in 1927 or 1928 we left Belorussia and traveled east by train to join Uncle Arkadiy and his wife. The luggage that we brought with us consisted of several bundles. It was all we owned. Uncle Arkadiy met us at the train station and helped father get a job in a village located near the railway station at Mauk, located north of Chelyabinsk. At first, father worked at a lumbering enterprise and then as an agronomist.

We lived in a building that was nothing more than a hut surrounded by a forest. The hut consisted of one room. We had a kitchen garden, some rabbits and some chickens to keep us alive. We were very poor, but then everyone in the Soviet Union at that time was poor.

In 1933 the country was struck by a famine which was called the Great Hunger. Mother brought my brother and me to Chelyabinsk and there the three of us lived in a small room in a communal apartment near the electric power station along the Mias River. With the assistance of Uncle Arkadiy, mother found a job working as a registration clerk in a clinic. It was not a high salary job.

In Chelyabinsk my brother and I attended a newly created school that was housed in a three-story building. It was established to accommodate the children of the men that built and operated the electric power station near Chelyabinsk. The teachers were brought to the school from other cities and a large percentage of them had been educated in Leningrad. All the teachers had received an excellent education and the ones from Leningrad were very familiar with the fine arts. The teachers taught us well. I still remember the teachers who taught me mathematics, physics, literature and history. In the ninth and tenth grades, I had a crush on my history teacher.

Later, much later, following my release from prison after Joseph Stalin's death, I was told that my former history teacher was working for the KGB (see Glossary- Soviet secret police). His name was Sergei Nikiforovich. I found his telephone number and called him. When we met, he told me that he had been aware of my arrest back in 1949 but had been powerless to help me.

In school I became involved in many different activities. I joined the literary circle, the dramatics circle and the chorus circle. I took guitar lessons, played volleyball and participated in planting trees in our district. I was also a conscientious student. Father had told my brother and me that because we were Jews it would be more difficult for us to become successful in society. In order for us to succeed, we would need to excel academically. We worked hard at our studies and were always on the academic honor roll. As two of the best students at the school, we were rewarded several times by the board of administrators of the electric power station. They gave us trips to Moscow, to the Caucasus Mountains and to the Crimea.

In tenth grade, I was elected the leader of the Komsomol organization of the school (see Glossary—Komsomol). It was 1937 and the NKVD was starting to arrest people who were accused of being "enemies of the people." (see Glossary—Soviet secret police) As the leader of the school's Komsomol organization it became my duty to remove from the organization the members who were the children of father's who were arrested and declared "enemies of the people." I was shocked that there were so many enemies within our area. Why were people suddenly so afraid of the NKVD? Why did people fear the arrival, during the night, of a truck or van and the sound of footsteps on the staircase?

["Enemy of the people" was a phrase applied to any opponent, real or imagined, of the Soviet Union. An "enemy of the people" was simply anyone so designated by the Soviet authorities. It was a phrase voiced by Stalin in his speeches following the assassination of Sergei Kirov in December 1934. The phrase became a Communist Party slogan; it was used by Party members as well as non-Party members. Most of those designated as "enemies of the people" were sentenced under Article 58 of the Criminal Code of the Russian Soviet Federated Socialist Republic, which was the Soviet Criminal Code. The code covered charges such as "wrecking," "espionage," "treason," and "anti-

Soviet agitation." Sentences for these "crimes" ranged from ten to twenty-five years of forced labor, or execution. "Enemy of the people" carried with it a stigma for the families of those declared as such. Wives and husbands of "enemies" were removed from their places of employment and residence. They were expelled from the Party and often also arrested. Children of "enemies" were denied entry into schools and universities and generally could find only the worst kinds of employment.]

One day a neighbor lady came to tell us that her husband had been arrested. She was terrified. Her husband was an engineer at the electric power station. She did not know for certain why he had been arrested. She supposed that it was because her husband had, years ago, fought for the White Army during the Russian Civil War. (see Appendix- Leon Trotsky and Trotskysim) My parents wondered why her husband had mentioned that in his written vitae. He could have left that out. But at that time people were honest and were used to telling the truth.

The chief engineer at the electric power station was also arrested. He was the father of my good friend, Artim. Everybody knew Artim and considered him an exemplary member of the school's Komsomol organization. Because his father had been arrested, I was told to expel Artim from the Komsomol organization. I felt it was wrong and went to see the chairman of the city's Komsomol Committee. I told him what I thought of Artim and that it was wrong to expel one of the organization's best members. The chairman sat in deep thought for a while and then replied that the "NKVD would not make a mistake." He said that they had discovered that Artim's father was an "enemy of the people." Artim, he said, was close to his father and must have known that his father was an "enemy of the people." Thus, he concluded, "Artim can not be a Komsomol member."

A short while later, the chairman of the city's Komsomol Committee was arrested by the NKVD. He too was charged with being an "enemy of the people." I realized then that the arrest of innocent people had become a new State policy. It was designed to terrorize the people [so that they would not dare criticize the State and its policies].

Chapter Five

Sofia

University Student

I decided to attend Leningrad State University long before I graduated from high school. Uncle Arkadiy had graduated from Leningrad Technological University and he told me about the beauty of Leningrad. I graduated from high school with such high scores that I was not required to take the university's entrance examinations.

I began my studies at the university in 1938. I attended the lectures of world famous academicians such as Yevgeniy Tarly, Peter Struve and Boris Grecov and I studied under excellent professors such as Vladislav Ravdonikas, Vladimir Mavrodin and Semyon Okun. When I came to know my professors, I realized that they were more than great historians; they were human beings after whom I could pattern my life.

I lived in the university's student housing located on the Fifth Line of Vasilievsky Island. There were three to four students in each room. We lived modestly. Our meals were simple. We ate our dinners at the university's canteen Number 8 and the meals consisted of soup and gruel. Of course, more attractive food was available at the canteen such as salamis and cheeses but we did not have the money to purchase it. We were given a monthly allowance of 24 rubles; only those who earned excellent grades received a monthly allowance.

Most of us were poor, very poor. We owned very few clothes. I wore blue overalls like the ones that the city cleaners wore. I had white linen gym shoes that I would clean using the powder with which I brushed my teeth. I also had an overcoat that had been made with the fabric of an old military coat. There were parties that were arranged by students but I didn't attend them because I did not have nice clothes. The professors at the university were also rather poor; in fact, everyone in our country suffered from poverty.

During my second year at the university, the Soviet Union went to war against Finland. It was announced by our government that the Finns had initiated the war. It was a lie and the State's lie became apparent after we learned that our country's military actions against Finland were being carried out in Finnish territory. Nevertheless, many university students voluntarily joined the army [the Red Army] in the fight against Finland.

After a while, a military hospital was organized in the building adjacent to the one used by the History Faculty. Many of the female students within the School of History worked as volunteers in the newly organized hospital. We saw many injured soldiers and a large percentage of these men suffered from injuries caused by the winter frost. The soldiers did not talk about the military developments or their actions along the front. I assume they were warned not to discuss the war with us.

The war began in November 1939 and ended in March 1940. We were kept informed about the military developments during the war by the government through radio broadcasts, through the newspapers and by way of film magazines, (they were all State controlled mediums). Initially, we believed the State controlled mediums. It never entered our minds to doubt the reports. I learned later that most of the reports were lies.

As a university student, I continued my work in the Komsomol organization. I tried to do everything that I could for other people. That was the principle which guided my behavior. I believe that treating others with kindness should be the guiding force within an individual. Kindness is most important. All other qualities such as a person's intellect, knowledge and optimism are not as important.

After I was elected to the Komsomol Committee within the School of History, I was made responsible for the moral behavior of all the students in the department. At one of the Komsomol meetings, the members discussed how a modern woman should dress. At another meeting we discussed the following question: "Is it moral or immoral for girls and boys to stay together in the same room for the night after a party?" At our meetings we would often denounce fascism. Thus, it was a shock when we were told in 1939 that Stalin had entered into an alliance with Adolf Hitler's fascist Germany.

We were shocked again when fascist Germany invaded the Soviet Union on June 22, 1941. It was a Sunday and I was visiting Uncle Arkadiy who had moved back to Leningrad from Chelyabinsk. We were listening to the radio when suddenly the voice of Vyacheslav Molotov, [Minister of Foreign Affairs of the Soviet Union] announced that fascist Germany had invaded our country.

The Soviet people were not naïve. We had been told and we believed that at some future date we would find ourselves at war. Our country was the world's only socialist state and it was surrounded by enemies. That is why the young people of our country had to pass specially created military exercises. The exercises were titled Be Ready to Work and Defend the USSR and they involved running, jumping, shooting a gun and throwing hand grenades. However, we did not expect to be attacked by fascist Germany. The people at large were under the impression that relations between Germany and the Soviet Union were good. After Stalin entered into an agreement with Hitler [a non-aggression pact signed on August 23, 1939], the word fascist was no longer used to describe Germany in radio broadcasts or in the newspapers.

Upon hearing that we had been invaded, I ran to the Komsomol Committee at the university to make myself available for volunteer work. The committee sent me and many other female students to the botanical garden of the university to dig trenches that were to be used as shelters during a bombardment or the shelling of the city. Thereafter, we were brought to an area a far distance away from the city to dig entrenchments and to build a military airport. [The airport was to be a flat open field.] Upon finishing our work, we were brought to other locations to dig entrenchments and prepare military airports. Each succeeding military airport was nearer to the outskirts of Leningrad because the German army was fast approaching the city. [Most likely each of the military airports would be used later by the German Luftwaffe after the German army captured and occupied the area south of the city.]

At the end of July 1941, some twenty-five students, including me, were sent by the Komsomol Committee to Daimishche, a village not far from Krasnoye Selo to prepare several secret military airports. [Krasnoye Selo is located some 30 kilometers or18.6 miles south of Leningrad.] We worked mainly at night to avoid being detected by German aircraft and our primary tools were spades.

By the end of August 1941, the Germans were approaching Gatchina. One morning, after we prepared to go to sleep having worked all night, we heard the sound of exploding shells nearby. When we heard the lowing of cows we went outside and saw many people and many cattle. They were going north to Leningrad. There were soldiers among the people and many of them were wounded. One of the soldiers had been a fellow student at the university. He informed us that they were retreating and that the fascists were not far behind. We realized that we needed to leave as well and so we joined the fleeing crowd and made our way to Krasnoye Selo. There, at the railway station, we boarded a train going to Leningrad. The train was filled to capacity. We were told later that it was the last Soviet train to leave Krasnoya Selo because the fascists had arrived at the city not more than an hour after we left.

When I arrived in Leningrad, I went to the city's Komsomol Committee and requested that I be sent to the military front as a trained nurse. My request was denied. I was sent instead, along with some other female university students, to a makeshift workshop to make artillery shells. At the workshop we worked with a number of women from various regions in the Leningrad Province. They had been evacuated when the fascists invaded the Soviet Union. We worked in one large hut [tent]. The women were stationed in one area of the workshop and we [the university students] worked in another area. Because we were more educated, we were given the more technical jobs. I don't know why, but I was appointed the leader of our so-called team.

The fascists began bombing Leningrad in September 1941. Walking down Nevsky Prospect one day, I could see men repairing the roof of the Book House [the largest and most popular book store in Leningrad]. Suddenly, I heard an explosion and I saw a "sack" with a red bottom fall from the roof of the building. Within seconds I realized that the "sack" was the body of a man. When I arrived at Palace Square [the square in front of the Winter Palace which had been renamed the Hermitage by the Russian Communists after they came to power], I saw that the building which was used by the Holy Synod of the High Orthodox Church was on fire. Walking along the embankment of the Neva River, I noticed that the windows of all the buildings facing the river had been turned into gun-posts for machine guns.

Leningraders were told that those who truly loved Leningrad would remain in the city. They would not leave but would defend the city from the approaching enemy. Thus, most Leningraders [even mothers with babies] refused to leave the city. It was a horrible mistake.

At night, during the aerial bombing of the city, one could see flares in the sky. People believed that the flares were being launched by fascist agents in Leningrad who were directing the German pilots to the most important military targets within the city. To make that assumption was understandable. However, to assume that a person was a German agent simply because he was wearing a white shirt and a tie was ridiculous. Such a person might become the victim of a crowd of people who accused him of aiding the enemy during the aerial bombing that had taken place the previous evening.

On October 1, 1941, I, along with twenty other female university students, was brought to a forest area in Medvezhy Stan. There, in a military workshop built on wheels, we put together artillery shells for anti-aircraft guns and for howitzers. We would take a used shell casing and pour into it the gunpowder. Then we coupled the shell casing to a high explosive shell and added a primer cap and a detonator. What we did was important but also very dangerous. We brought the finished shells to a railway car that was parked some 60 to 70 meters [197 feet to 230 feet] from the workshop. It was so cold [minus 40 degrees Celsius in the suburbs of Leningrad] that we decided that no one should be out in the open air for longer than ten minutes at a time. Periodically, soldiers would arrive at our workshop directly from the military front. They would pick up a load of finished shells and bring them to their military battery where they were used almost immediately.

We worked with "old" soldiers. We thought they were elderly but they were only thirty to forty years old, but because we were so young they seemed to us to be "old men." During the early weeks of our work at Medvezhy Stan, we were fed delicious vegetable soup and gruel every day. The meals were a great improvement over the meals we ate as university students. But after the fascists established a blockade against Leningrad our meals became progressively worse. (see Glossary—Siege of Leningrad) Some of the soldiers we worked with died from starvation. We were young and tried to remain optimistic. We did this by singing and dancing.

In November [1941], I was given a day off and I decided to visit my brother who was stationed at an anti-aircraft battery inside Leningrad. [Sofia's brother was drafted into military service just before the invasion of the Soviet Union in 1941.] I was given a ride by a truck driver who was headed for Leningrad. What I witnessed when we entered the city was truly shocking. Many buildings had been destroyed. I saw people who could barely walk, people who were pulling sleds that carried their dead relatives and people getting water from a hole made in the ice that covered the Neva River. With great difficulty, I found my brother's battery. I was so happy to see him. I was also surprised to see that the men in his battery were using artillery shells that had been made in our workshop. The boxes in which the shells were transported bore our stamp.

After the war, I received a letter from the mother of one of the girls in my work brigade [team] at Medvezhy Stan. The girl's name was Lena Sozanskaya and her mother wrote that she thanked God every day that He [God] had chosen me, during the war, to be her daughter's guardian and the guardian of other female university students. She claimed that I had protected them from frost, from hunger and ultimately from death. I appreciated the remarks, but I do not believe it was me that helped her daughter and the others survive. I think it was our friendship plus our belief in our country's future victory that helped us survive the cold temperatures and starvation.

In March 1942, Leningrad State University was evacuated to the city of Saratov. I, along with many other university students, was brought to the western side of Lake Ladoga. From there we were transported by trucks across the ice covered lake to the eastern side. Fortunately, the fascists did not attack us from the air, but we did see much evidence of previous attacks. We drove past lorries [trucks] that had been bombed and were turned into motionless charred corpses. We saw large holes in the ice through which lorries, carrying people, had disappeared. When we arrived in Borisova Grivah, along the eastern side of the lake, we were fed. We were so hungry that the dry pieces of bread that we were given seemed fantastically delicious.

From Lake Ladoga we were transported to Saratov by train. Our university professors were appointed the supervisors of each train car. Professor Sergei Kuznetzov, the Dean of the faculty of the School of Geology, was placed in charge of all the students as well as the professors on the train. He was very kind, considerate and responsible. Later, Professor Kuznetzov would describe the train trip in his memoirs. He wrote:

"All the students and professors on the train were weak from hunger. They were so weak that it was almost impossible for them to lift their luggage into the train cars to which they were assigned. Some of the luggage was never brought into the train; it was left in the snow. When the chief conductor of the train was asked to delay the train's departure, he replied that this was not possible because fascist pilots had already spotted the train and they would soon be bombing the train. An enemy airplane did appear and dropped several bombs, but none hit the intended target. Most of the people on the train were not aware of the enemy attack; they had fallen asleep shortly after the train started to move."

The train arrived in Saratov ten days later. Sofia recalled that when the citizens of Saratov saw the people get off the train, they wept. "We looked worse than human corpses. Many of us were immediately hospitalized. Several girls died shortly after they entered the hospital."

The university was housed in the hotel "Russia" in Saratov. The rooms of the first floor were turned into offices and the professors and a number of students were placed on the second floor. The remaining students were assigned to hostels in the city. The class sizes were small. The professors would deliver their lectures to groups of four or five students within the rooms where the professors or the students lived. We knew our professors very well back in Leningrad and we respected them. They were people of highest culture. But in Saratov, since we lived together in such close quarters, we saw sides of their personalities that were new to us. There were two washrooms in the hotel, but one of them broke. As a result, the professors and their families and the students had to share the same washroom. Two lines were formed at the door of the washroom. Three women and then three men would take turns entering the washroom to use the toilette inside.

It was Professor Voznesensky, the Rector of Leningrad State University, who saved the university. It was he who saved the professors and students from the starvation which took the lives of hundreds of thousands of people in blockaded Leningrad. It was he who organized the evacuation of the university to Saratov [not to the Caucasus as Moscow had recommended]. It was he that organized the university's return to Leningrad after the German blockade against Leningrad was brought to an end. This was accomplished with great effort on his part. It also helped that the Rector's brother was a member of the government in Moscow.

Our good Rector tried to make sure that all the students' needs were met as quickly as possible. I witnessed the assistance that he gave to Aita, a female student from Estonia. Aita's mother had been Sergei Kirov's secretary in Leningrad. After Kirov's assassination, Aita's mother was arrested and banished to a prison labor camp where she died. Aita was a beautiful girl but she was very poor. When we arrived in Saratov, she was wearing a sack in which she had made three holes, one for her head and two for her arms. She had no shoes or boots so she walked around barefoot. When our good Rector saw Aita, he approached her and asked her in a very considerate manner her name and her major area of study. A few days later, Aita was invited to the Rector's office where she was given a voucher for a new dress and for foot wear.

There were several guys among the students. Most of them were ill but some were not, though they claimed that they were. The latter had avoided military service by lying to the authorities, pretending to be ill. However, no one suspected that they had lied. We truly believed that they were ill. One of these guys was Peter Grigoriev. [After the war, in 1949, he would slander Sofia during a MGB investigation.]

Grigoriev already had a less than honorable history. He had spent some time in a prison labor camp located along the Belomor Canal [by the White Sea]. We assumed that he was sent there because his father, a wealthy peasant farmer, was arrested in the early 1930s. [Grigoriev's father was a kulak.] Grigoriev was so different from the rest of us; he was older and much more independent and street smart. In the evenings, the electricity in Saratov was turned off. So the professors and students made small kerosene lamps and used them for light. Grigoriev, however, was able to purchase a large kerosene lamp and he invited students to sit around his large lamp and read into the night. The students who used his lamp, had to pay him. There was a monetary fee. We had never before witnessed the likes of Grigoriev. When rumor had it that Grigoriev had eaten the flesh of a dead woman during the days of severe hunger in Leningrad, we did not doubt the rumor.

None of the students were well dressed. I came to Saratov wearing blue overalls and I wore them during the entire time [two years] that the university's activities were conducted in Saratov. It was the good Rector again who provided those who were in need with better clothes. He was able to acquire unbleached calico trousers and padded jackets lined with warm padding. He was also able acquire many boots with wooden soles. It was the duty of the Students' Trade Union at the university to distribute the clothes and boots to the students who needed them most.

The Students' Trade Union and the University Komsomol Committee were two important student organizations at Leningrad State University. Olga Fishman was the leader of the University Komsomol Committee and I was elected to lead the Students' Trade Union. It was my responsibility to make sure that every student had proper accommodations and was fed and clothed and had footwear. In the winter of 1942–1943, the heating system of one of the hostels used by the university to house students stopped functioning. I had to move the students in that hostel to another one. When our good

Rector was given permission to take wood for fuel from the barges that traveled on the Volga River, the Students' Trade Union organized student teams to remove the wood that was needed from the barges. I actively participated in the work assignments organized by the Students' Trade Union and considered them fun activities.

During the summer vacation almost all the students were brought to collective farms to work. It was Professor Voznesensky's idea. The good Rector wanted us to help the collective farm workers and he believed that the students, by living on a collective farm, would have a better diet; we would eat more vegetables. When I and others arrived at the collective farm to which we were assigned, we discovered that the members of the collective farm were poor and that their diet was no better than ours as students. Before the war, this collective farm was peopled by ethnic Germans. With the outbreak of the war, the ethnic Germans in our collective farm and in the farms throughout the Volga River area were forced to move to Siberia. [They were moved within twenty-four hours and were forced to leave behind most of their personal possessions.] (see Glossary—Collective Farm)

The Soviet government repopulated the collective farms with Ukrainians. We assisted them in a variety of tasks, with whatever needed to be done. We planted wheat, we harvested the wheat and we delivered the wheat to the government owned silos. We used bulls to pull to the silos the open carts filled with wheat. At the silos we shoveled the wheat in sacks and then we climbed to the top of the silos to dump the wheat into the silos. It was hard work.

Sometimes camels were used to bring the wheat grain to the government silos. Our bulls had never before seen camels. They became so frightened that they would rush to the side of the road causing the open cart full of grain to tip and fall on its side. All the grain had to be picked up and that took a long time.

Shortly after the summer vacation ended and the students returned to Saratov, the Students' Trade Union was faced with a serious problem. The problem concerned a newly enrolled student who had arrived from Warsaw where he had lived in the Jewish Ghetto. He had escaped from the ghetto. He was as thin as a pole. He was always hungry. He could not stop eating the wheat that we had brought with us from the collective farms. As a consequence, he suffered a stomach ailment and it was necessary to get him to the hospital quickly. But where could I get a car to transport him? I went looking for Rector Voznesensky but he wasn't at the university. I was told that he was attending a District Party Committee meeting. I telephoned the place where the committee was meeting and I was able to communicate the problem to the good Rector. He sent his car immediately to our hostel to help the young man. The Rector's decision reflected his character; he was a kind man.

When the fascists approached the city of Stalingrad, just 482 kilometers [300 miles] south of Saratov, several female students left the university and volunteered to defend Stalingrad. I remember accompanying them to the railway station and expressing my best wishes for them. We knew that the future of our country depended on the outcome of the battle for Stalingrad. One of the student volunteers was Marxena Elyashova. (Marxena along with her sister Ludmila Elyashova became Sofia's friends after the war.)

Marxena Elyashova was also a friend of the authors. She told them that when she and her female companions arrived in Stalingrad, the battle for the city was already in progress. They were housed together in a separate room in one of the military barracks used by the soldiers. They were supplied with

Figure 5.1. Marxena Elyashova in military uniform at Stalingrad. Courtesy of Alexey Vinogradov.

warm military trousers, military overcoats, fur caps and felt boots. They were assigned to various duties.

Marxena was trained initially to be a radio operator. Later her commanding officer decided that she should become a topography calculator. [Such a person uses topographical instruments to determine the distances of ground targets. That information is then used by the men operating the artillery.] When Marxena's commander learned that she did not like her new assignment, he ordered that she be brought to his dugout. While the commander was explaining the importance of her new job, he was interrupted by one of his officers who burst into the dugout to announce: "Our troops have taken the Tractor Mills [the last stronghold of the Germans in Stalingrad]. All of Stalingrad is ours!"

During the clearing of Stalingrad, Marxena and her female companions were assigned to look through the city's rubble for military weapons that had been left behind by the enemy. In her search, Marxena was exposed to thousands of human corpses and all of them were enemy soldiers; the Soviet soldiers killed during battle had already been removed. Fortunately, it was winter and decomposition had not yet begun. As Marxena looked upon the corpses, she noticed that death had drained from the bodies the color of life. Marxena saw one young German soldier lying on his back with outstretched arms as if he had been crucified. As she looked at his face, she could see that his beautiful blue eyes were directed toward the sky. "Immediately, an overwhelming sadness rose within me," Marxena recollected. She no longer considered the dead soldier lying before her an enemy but a precious human being whose life had been taken from him by the actions of war.

In January 1943 the blockade against Leningrad ended as the Soviet troops pushed the fascists back and away from the city. When we were informed about this military development, Sofia recalled, we were so happy and began dreaming of returning to our beautiful city. I was one of fourteen people sent to Leningrad to make ready the university buildings and the student living quarters before the others arrived from Saratov. We discovered that the university buildings were in terrible condition and the inside walls needed to be re-plastered. We were taught the skill of plastering and we worked hard trying to repair the damaged walls. In fact, most of the students who returned from Saratov took part in the reparations.

Chapter Six

Sofia

Arrested and Sentenced

The two years that followed the end of the Great Patriotic War were marked with wonderful developments. I married Nikolai Firsov, a returning soldier who had lost his right hand during the war. I was elected the leader of the University Komsomol Committee. In 1947, I finished my post graduate courses and defended my doctoral dissertation on Georgy Plekhanov. [Plekhanov was one of the first Marxists in Tsarist Russia; he was the leader of the international socialist movement.] After I defended my dissertation, I was given a teaching position as an assistant lecturer within the Faculty of Economics at Leningrad State University. Everything was excellent in my life. I loved my husband and I liked my job and my colleagues. Plus, I lived in a country that had just won a war and defeated fascism.

The Faculty of Economics at the university was established before the war in 1939. The first head of the department was our Rector, Professor Voznesensky. He brought into the department Anthony Bukovetsky, Jacob Rozenfeldt, Victor Reichardt and Victor Shtein.

Anthony Bukovetsky had been a consultant on economic matters to the Russian Duma from 1911 to 1914. Later he became one of the major contributors that designed the State Bank of the Soviet Union. Professor Bukovetsky did not like the Soviet government but he was never an outspoken enemy of the regime. He was a very good professor and was assigned to be one of the critics of my dissertation during the defense of my dissertation. Professor Bukovetzky was arrested in the late 1940s. I do not know why; I can only speculate and it is my guess that he was accused of "cosmopolitanism."

Jacob Rozenfeldt was a leading authority on Marxism as it relates to economics. In the late 1940s, he authored a book on the history of America's industry. In it he described America's aid to the Soviet Union during the Great Patriotic War. The contents of the book, especially America's aid to the Soviet Union, as well as Rozenfeldt's trips abroad would be used to justify his arrest. He was declared guilty of the charges that were brought against him. He died shortly after he served his prison sentence.

Victor Reichardt like Professor Rozenfeldt was an authority on Marxism and how it should be applied to economics. He authored a short book in which he described ancient social relations based on Marxist methodology. The booklet was translated into Japanese which became grounds for his arrest. He was accused of being a spy for Japan. At the time of his arrest, he was the Dean of the Faculty of Economics. He was a kind man who had a tender disposition. His lectures on the history of economic systems were very interesting. Professor Reichardt was declared guilty of the charge brought against him and was sent to a prison in Moscow. Later his wife and his young daughter were also arrested and they too were sent to a prison in Moscow. Professor Reichardt would die in prison on November 16, 1949.

Professor Victor Shtein, like Professor Bukovetsky, was a member of the committee which reviewed my dissertation. He was very knowledgeable and spoke several European and Oriental languages. He had worked for a long time in China as an advisor on economics to the Chinese government. He was the Dean of the faculty that taught Oriental languages. His ancestors were Jews, but he had been baptized in the Russian Orthodox Church. I visited him at his home. It was a large apartment not far from Nevsky Prospect. The entire apartment had belonged to his father before the Bolshevik Revolution. After the Bolsheviks [later they called themselves Communists] came to power, the apartment was turned into a communal dwelling. Professor Shtein and his family occupied three rooms and four or five other families lived in the remaining rooms. Nevertheless, Professor Shtein had a large study which held a large collection of books. I was told that following the arrest of Professor Shtein, his enemies within the Oriental language faculty acquired his personal library, a truck full of books, at a very low price.

Professor Shtein was arrested in 1948 and the charge was "cosmopolitanism." He had just authored a book entitled *Economic and Political Concepts in Russia in the Nineteenth Century*. Following the book's publication, it was awarded an important prize from Leningrad State University. But shortly after Professor Shtein was given the award, the State dictated that "cosmopolitanism" was to be condemned by everyone; it became a new State policy. Professor Shtein was accused of being "cosmopolitan" for two reasons. In his book he pointed out the Western influences on the economic and political developments in Russia during the nineteenth century. That was the first reason. The second reason was the absence of Joseph Stalin's name. The leader of the Soviet Union was not mentioned in the book.

In June 1948 members of the Communist Party within the Faculty of Economics called a special meeting to discuss Professor Shtein's recently published book. They urged the professors and the young instructors in the department to denounce Professor Shtein and his book. The young instructors were those who had finished their postgraduate courses but had not yet written a doctoral dissertation. Among the instructors there were S. Mikheyeva, N. Moiseyenko and Peter Grigoriev [the same Grigoriev who Sofia came to know as a student in Saratov]. The instructors planned to use the new State's policy against "cosmopolitanism" to advance their own careers. The leader of this group was Seraphim Ilyin, an agronomist who had been brought into the Faculty of Economics to lecture on the economics of agriculture. After joining the department, Ilyin became the school's representative within the university's Faculty Communist Party Bureau. Ilyin had also become the Deputy Dean of the Faculty of Economics.

Twenty speakers were scheduled to make comments about Professor Shtein's recently published book at an upcoming meeting. I was asked to speak at the meeting since I was one of the younger instructors who had earned a Ph.D. I was told that I would be the last speaker. The nineteen speakers before me had been told to denounce the professor and his book. I was not told what to say but I assume that Ilyin and the other Communist Party members were sure that I too would denounce Professor Shtein and his book. They were sure that I would not dare refute the other speakers.

I agreed to be a speaker but I preferred not to speak. I knew that if I listened to my conscience and obeyed it, my comments might jeopardize my future. Yet, I knew that I could not refuse to speak because it would cause them to suspect me of supporting Professor Shtein and his book. I became extremely nervous as I waited for my turn to speak. Each of the speakers before me denounced Professor Shtein. A large proportion of them denounced him with great enthusiasm. Some, I noticed, did so with hesitation; it was obvious that they were too afraid to voice their inner convictions, so they lied to save themselves.

I could not lie. When it was my turn to speak, I stood up and announced that "I would like to criticize our critics!" I then explained that all the speakers before me had misrepresented the contents of Professor Shtein's book; they had distorted the professor's words; they had all voiced an agreed upon lie. When I finished, there were some at the meeting who applauded my remarks. My husband was at the meeting and I could see that all the color in his face was gone; he looked as white as a linen sheet. Professor Shtein was also at the meeting. He did not try to defend himself or his writings. He knew all about the MGB which had replaced the NKVD because back in 1937 the NKVD had arrested him and he had spent some time in prison. The events at the meeting of denunciation were recorded and later my comments at the meeting would be used against me by the MGB. (see Glossary—Soviet secret police)

Most of the people who were present at the meeting of denunciation, kept their silence. Everyone, almost everyone, in the Soviet Union had witnessed the Great Terror of the 1930s. They knew it was dangerous to come to a person's defense if that person was accused of violating a State policy. It was much easier and safer to be among those who attacked a person that was being accused of being an "enemy of the people."

Many years later, in March 1988, Leningrad State University celebrated the memory of Professor Voznesensky, our former Rector. [Professor Voznesensky was arrested in 1949 and was shot in 1950.] Present at the celebration were some of those who had denounced not only Professor Shtein in 1948 but other faculty members as well in 1949. At the celebration they tried to justify what they had done back forty and forty-one years ago. They claimed that they had been ordered by the Communist Party to fight against "cosmopolitanism." I was at the celebration and when I heard their remarks I stood up and asked them, "Was it the Communist Party that ordered you to lie? Was it the MGB that ordered you to kill professors and put them in prison? Who namely ordered you to kill your professors?"

Elections were held at the university in 1949. Faculty members were to be elected to the Faculty Communist Party Bureau. In order to be the lead faculty member [the Dean] within a Faculty [of a school such as the School of Economics], one had to be a member of the Faculty Communist Party Bureau. Professor Reichardt was the Dean of the School of Economics and he was also a member of the Faculty Communist Party Bureau. Seraphim Ilyin, who was already the Deputy Dean of the School of Economics, wanted to replace Professor Reichardt and become the acting Dean. To achieve this aim, Ilyin applied huge efforts to persuade the faculty to vote against Professor Reichardt in the professor's bid to remain a member of the Faculty Communist Party Bureau. Elections were held and Professor Reichardt was reelected; he remained the School of Economics' acting Dean.

Ilyin then spread the rumor that the election results had been falsified. Since I was the head of the election commission which was responsible for counting the votes, the rumor was designed to slander me as well. I denied the rumor. I explained that during the evening of the day of the election, the vote ballots were collected and the election commission then, as one body, went to a separate room to count them. I divided the ballots among the six members of the commission and they in turn gave me the election results. I did not look at the names on the ballots. I added up the ballots and placed them in a large envelope; it was done in the presence of the entire election commission. Then, we, the members of the election commission, returned to the hall where the faculty members were waiting for the election results. I announced the election results and handed the large envelope containing the ballots to Ilyin, the Deputy Dean.

Later the Regional Party Committee invited me to appear before them. They told me that Ilyin insisted that I had falsified the results of the election. I denied it and each member of the election commission testified that I had not tampered with the ballots.

Ilyin's campaign to acquire the position of acting Dean of the School of Economics would succeed in time. Professor Reichardt was excluded from the Communist Party and was fired. The faculty members that had supported Professor Reichardt were released by Leningrad State University and reassigned to other universities. I was also reassigned and became an assistant lecturer at the Leningrad Electrical Engineering University.

One day, I met a former colleague who kept his faculty position at Leningrad State University. It was he who informed me that Professor Reichardt had been excluded from the Communist Party. He said that the professor had not been invited to the meeting in which it was decided he should be removed from the Party. "Why didn't you notify the Professor about the meeting?," I asked. My former colleague replied that one had to be very careful considering the existing situation within the School of Economics. One could easily lose his or her job. His reply angered me and I retorted, "You are a scoundrel like all the others!" I then walked away.

I visited Professor Reichardt after he lost his job at the university. I may have been the only person from the university to visit him. My husband tried to discourage me from associating with Professor Reichardt. He felt that to associate with the professor would hurt my career. I understood my husband's concern and I would learn later that the MGB was watching me and monitoring my actions.

In May, Professor Reichardt was arrested and soon thereafter Professor Shtein was arrested as well as some others who I knew. Professor Reichardt would die while being interrogated.

I suspected that I too would be arrested. I was pregnant at the time and wondered what would happen to my baby if I should be sent to prison. I tried not to dwell on that prospect and as a distraction I would visit museums, go to the theater and walk through the city's parks. One day, as I walked through the forested area along the shore of the Gulf of Finland, I said "good-bye" to the trees and the beautiful nature among the trees. By that time I believed my arrest was inevitable.

In July 1949, I went to visit my parents who lived in Viritza, some 80 kilometers [fifty miles] from Leningrad. That evening a man came to my parents' house; he wanted to see our passports [internal passports]. We wondered who this man was and why he asked to see our passports. Later it became clear to us; that same evening agents of the MGB had gone to my apartment [on Marat Prospect] in Leningrad to arrest me. My neighbors had told the agents that they were sure that I had gone to Viritza to visit my parents. (see Glossary—Soviet secret police)

The next morning agents of the MGB arrived at my parents' house and arrested me. It was July 13, 1949. The agents escorted me to a black car and brought me to my apartment in Leningrad. With the assistance of the apartment building supervisor, the agents searched my apartment. They found several old magazines that dated back to the 1920s. The magazines belonged to my husband's uncle who had managed a used book store. The magazines contained articles written by Leon Trotsky and others who had been condemned as "enemies of the people." The agents were not interested in my lectures or the articles that I had written. The search lasted some two hours. (see Appendix—Leon Trotsky and Trotskyism)

Following the search, the agents placed me in a "Black Raven" and transported me to the Bolshoy Dom [Big House] of the MGB on Liteiny Prospect. The "Black Raven" was a black vehicle consisting of two compartments, the driver's cab at the front and a large van at the rear. The only door to the van was at the rear. The only window to the van was near the top of the rear door, and in front of the window there were steel bars. Inside, there were two long benches, one along each side of the van. The benches must have been a new edition because during the Great Terror [or Great Purge] of 1937–1938, the inner space of a "Black Raven" van consisted of small enclosed boxes each used to hold one person. The NKVD agents who conducted the arrests during the Great Terror would transport several people in a "Black Raven" van and they did not want the victims to communicate with each other. As I was being transported to the Bolshoy Dom, I felt relieved. The long awaited arrest had finally come.

The days of confinement in the Bolshoy Dom were very difficult. Upon my arrival, they searched me and then they took photographs of me. It was a humiliating experience. I was then brought to a solitary confinement cell which was no larger than five meters long and two meters wide [15 feet by 6.5 feet]. There was a high small iron-barred window within the rear wall of the cell. On the outside, the window was covered with a boxlike shell which allowed some light to enter the cell but it prevented the detainee within the cell from seeing any activity outside. The cell was furnished with an iron bed which was to be used only at night. Early each morning it was to be folded up and was to remain folded until the evening. I was five months pregnant but I was permitted to use the bed only at night. During the night, the cell was illuminated with a bright light that was located directly above my head. The light could not be switched off within the cell. I could not cover my face because I was ordered to keep my arms on the blanket. There was a special peephole in the door of the cell so that a prison guard could watch my every movement.

I had read the accounts of people who had been sentenced to prison. I remembered reading about Felix Dzerzhinsky (the leader of CHEKA) and how he had remained active doing physical exercises while he was in prison. I decided that I would do that as well believing that it would be good for the baby that I was carrying. One of the guards noticed it and ordered me to stop exercising. The guard must have been watching me through the peephole in the door.

Several days after my arrival, I was brought before a group of MGB agents. The officer in the group informed me that I was being charged with high treason due to my active participation in a Trotskyite organization. (see Appendix—Leon Trotsky and Trotskyism) I told them that the accusation was false and that they should talk to my students and other people who knew me well. They would tell them that I was not a Trotskyite. The officer replied, "You should ask your lawyer later to use these people as witnesses for your defense during your trial." I then asked the officer what I had done specifically that caused them to label me a Trotskyite. He pondered for a minute and then asked, "What is Trotskyism?" I responded by explaining to him Trotskyism. He was unfamiliar with what I told him and I realized he was not well educated. He was not well versed in our country's laws. [The MGB officer should have been familiar with Trotskyism. It was described and explained in detail in the Great Soviet Encyclopedia published in 1947, two years before Sofia's arrest.] (see Document Two)

In preparation for my defense, I asked a guard to bring me books that were written by Vladimir Lenin. The guard responded with an ironic smile, "Why do you, an 'enemy of the people' want to read Lenin?" Nevertheless, I was brought the writings of Lenin. I was brought a different book each week from the prison library. The books were rather old. I think the library dated back to pre-revolutionary times.

I did not suffer from loneliness during the early weeks of my imprisonment. I kept busy reading and I read a lot. I pondered my future and the future of my country. I took short walks in a small section within the prison yard. For a short while, I was joined in my cell with another woman. She was a distant relative of Sergei Kamenev [who had been Commander-in-Chief of the Red Army during the Russian Civil War].

The child growing within me was a constant concern. There were nights when I simply could not sleep. Upon the recommendation of the prison doctor, I was permitted to sleep for one hour during the day. Due to my pregnancy and because I was not supplied with vitamins, I suffered from a toothache. I asked my relatives to supply me with carrots, but they were permitted to send me only two kilograms of items per month. In November [1949], they sent me some clothes and a blanket for my future baby.

The MGB interrogations continued into November. Sometimes they were conducted at night. A guard would escort me from my cell at midnight and I would not return until around 6:00 A.M. On the walk to the interrogation room and then back to my cell, I was required to hold my hands behind my back. I found it difficult to do because of my condition; I was pregnant, carrying a child. The guard would yell at me to walk faster but I told him I couldn't walk any faster. He retorted, that I should have thought about that earlier [before committing a crime against the State].

During the interrogations, the prosecutor representing the State used two witnesses to testify against me. They were S. Mikheyeva and Peter Grigoriev. Mikheyeva was one of the young instructors at Leningrad State University; she had finished her post-graduate courses but had not written a doctoral dissertation. She accused me of being a Zionist. (see Appendix—Political Zionism) She claimed that she had heard me remark, on two occasions, that I thought it was a shame that the anti-Semitism prevalent in the Soviet Union made it difficult for Jews to earn postgraduate degrees. Grigoriev testified that he had heard me, back in Saratov during the war, tell an anecdote about Soviet society which was quite derogatory. He concluded his testimony by turning to me and saying, "Now you will see what life is like in a prison camp!" I was told later that Mikheyeva and Grigoriev were also used by the State to "expose" and then convict other university faculty members.

The original Faculty of Economics was eventually entirely removed. Ilyin became the Dean of the Faculty of Economics and he also became the head of the School of Political Economics. Later, he would become the Deputy Rector of the entire university. The young instructors who supported Ilyin in his endeavors and who helped him gain his positions within the university, finished their doctoral dissertations rather quickly and awarded each other with degrees. I doubt that they furthered the progress of science and I am sure that their students did not benefit from their work.

On November 24, [1949], I began to experience labor pains. It was decided that I should be brought to Leningrad's infamous prison called "Kresty" [Crosses] because the prison included a hospital. I was transported to "Kresty" in a "Black Raven" and when we arrived I was brought to a large common cell without windows and without ventilation. The cell was crowded with men and women. The prison guards then went in search of a solitary confinement cell in which I could give birth. Meanwhile, the labor pains continued and I feared I was going to give birth in the crowded, dark and dirty cell and without medical aid. Finally, a man within the cell grabbed the iron cover of the pot that was used as a toilet and with it started beating the door with it shouting: "The woman is giving birth! Stop this vicious mockery of human suffering!" The prison door opened and a guard led me to a solitary confinement cell. It was a narrow dark cell with dirty walls. Chained to one of the walls was an iron baby cradle. When I saw what was to be my baby's cradle, I broke down and began crying. Four months had gone by since my arrest and I had tried to remain strong. But seeing the iron cradle was just too much for me to bear. It was the first time that I cried as a prisoner.

I gave birth to my baby in the prison hospital. It was not a difficult birth but I was weak. I was assisted by a midwife who was both rude and insensitive. As she assisted me, she told me that she had read an article in *Leningrad Pravda* (the city newspaper controlled by the State) and it concerned the Faculty of Economics at the university. She asked what I had done to become an "enemy of the people?"

When I gave birth to my child, I saw a small pale baby boy. He was so weak that he could barely cry. I was brought to the prison hospital ward and there I joined more than ten other women who had recently given birth. They were called "mamkas" which was prison slang for the word "mothers." These women were criminals but they were very kind towards me. They would assist me whenever I needed help. Later, after they were moved from the hospital ward, they would secretly visit me.

We were handed our babies every three hours in order to feed them and were given thirty minutes to feed them. My baby was so weak that he would fall asleep before I could fill him with the milk of my breast. He began losing weight. Thank God, the prison doctor ordered that I be moved to another ward where I could stay with my baby all day long, otherwise my baby would have died. The doctor also recommended that I walk for forty minutes each day in the prison yard with my baby.

Two months later, I was moved to a prison cell which was already inhabited by a woman who had also given birth while in prison. She was the daughter-in-law of Leonid Nikolayev. [He was executed on December 29, 1934. He was charged with and found guilty of murdering Sergei Kirov who was assassinated on December 1, 1934. Kirov was the Party leader in Leningrad.] Leonid's daughter-in-law, the woman with whom I was now sharing a prison cell, was only ten years old when her father-in-law was executed.

Before the date of my trial, I was permitted to read a description of the State's case against me. I was astonished that two of my friends were going to be used to testify against me. They had decided to betray me. The first was Elisabeth Anisimova, whose portrait had been placed next to mine as the two best students within the School of Economics. She claimed that I had tried to persuade her to change her dissertation topic; the title of her dissertation was "Industrialization in the USSR." Elisabeth was right; I felt that her dissertation topic was too broad but that, however, is what she failed to mention. Thus, my comment to her could be interpreted as being unpatriotic. The second person scheduled to testify against me would report that I had criticized him for not notifying Professor Reichardt about the meeting in which those who were present evicted the professor from the Communist Party. [This was true and Sofia had called that person a scoundrel. The fact that

Sofia had voiced sympathy towards Professor Reichardt is what would be used against her.]

I soon learned that there was to be no trial. It was the prison warden who informed me of this development after I was escorted to a corridor within the prison. He read to me the following verdict: "For your active role in propaganda against the Soviet Union, in Trotskyism and in Zionism, the Special Council according to Article 58 paragraph 10 condemns you for 10 years."

[Article 58 was the first article in the "Specific Section" of the Criminal Code of the Russian Soviet Federated Socialist Republic. The 1934 version of the Criminal Code was divided into two parts: the "General Section" which included Articles 1 through 57 and the "Specific Section" which included Articles 58 through 205. The "Specific Section" named specific crimes and penalties for violations. Article 58 paragraph 10 reads as follows:

> "Propaganda or agitation, containing a call for the overthrow, subversion, or weakening of Soviet authority or for the carrying out of other counterrevolutionary crimes, and likewise the distribution or preparation or keeping of literature of this nature shall be punishable by deprivation of liberty for a term not less than six months. The same actions during mass disturbances, or with the use of religious or nationalist prejudices of the masses, or in a war situation, or in areas proclaimed to be in a war situation, shall be punishable by measures of social defense, indicated in Article 58 paragraph 2 of this code."]

When the warden finished reading the sentence, I began to laugh. I was laughing at myself for being so naive as to believe that I was going to be given a genuine trial. I was laughing at myself for having spent time and energy preparing for my defense. It had already been decided that I was to be sentenced to prison for ten years even if I was innocent of treason.

Later, while serving my term in a prison labor camp, I learned that many of my inmates had not received a trial. They told me that they were brought before two or three MGB officers who read to them the crime or crimes for which they were being sentenced to prison. They were not provided with legal counsel or a lawyer. They were not permitted to ask any questions. After they were read their sentence, they were escorted away.

One old woman in the prison labor camp told me that she was serving a twenty-five year prison sentence. She was charged with and found guilty of "attempting to assassinate Stalin." The charge stemmed from the fact that she had burned a newspaper which included Stalin's portrait.

At this time, from 1947 to 1950, there was no death penalty in the Soviet Union; it had been abolished. So during those three years many people who were declared guilty of committing a crime were given long prison sentences. The following is one of many anecdotes told by prisoners at that time: One day, a prison warden had all of his prisoners brought outside to stand in formation in several long lines. He then called upon those who had short sentences to step forward. None of the prisoners stepped forward. The warden then addressed a prisoner by the name of Ivanov. "What is your sentence Ivanov?" "Ten years," Ivanov answered. "You son of a bitch," the warden yelled, "why the Hell didn't you step forward?"

I would remain in the prison called "Kresty" until they transported me to my final destination, a prison labor camp in the North. In "Kresty" I was given visitation privileges and my relatives did come to visit me. It was difficult to communicate in the visitation room because the room was divided into two sections. The prisoners would sit in one section and the visitors sat in the other section. The sections were separated from each other with two metal latticed fences and a two-meter wide alley between the two fences. Several prisoners and their relatives would be in the room at the same time which made it noisy. To hear each other, it was necessary to speak loudly. [There was virtually no privacy.] During one of the visits, my husband told me "I'm sure that you are innocent. I'll be waiting for you." I believed him.

Chapter Seven

Sofia

Exiled to a Prison Labor Camp

Without any advanced notice I was released from "Kresty" and transported to a prison labor camp. It was the beginning of March 1950. The trip to the prison labor camp and my life at the camp would be very difficult. Thus, I find it difficult to talk about this time in my life, yet I must. I believe that others should know what happened to me and to the millions of Soviet citizens who were sent to work in Stalin's prison labor camps. A large percentage of these prisoners were innocent of violating Soviet laws.

The train that was used to transport me and many other prisoners from Leningrad to Vologda consisted of "Stolypin carriages." The doors to these carriages could not be opened; they were held shut with metal bars. The windows were firmly closed. There were separate compartments in each carriage and sixteen prisoners were placed in each compartment. There were six berths in a compartment which meant that several persons had to sit on a berth. Among the prisoners in my compartment there was a child not older than three years. His mother was a criminal from the western part of Ukraine. The little boy was clever. He asked for permission and was given permission by our guard to leave the compartment and run up and down the carriage corridor.

The other child within our compartment was my baby. He was weak and frail but I had no food to give him because our departure from Leningrad had come so suddenly. My parents were unable to supply me with food before I left Leningrad.

We changed trains in Vologda. At the railway station the prisoners were ordered to stand in line, it was a long line, and we were marched to the prison at Vologda. There were guards with dogs on both sides of the line. I carried my baby in my arms and the woman from western Ukraine carried my luggage. As we approached the Vologda prison, I noticed a large inscription on one of the walls of the building. The inscription was covered with paint but it was still legible. It read "Cursed is the individual who believes that prison can rehabilitate a person." (see Glossary—Soviet rehabilitation)

The next day, early, we continued our journey to the north and east. After several days of travel, the train stopped in an open field covered with snow and we were ordered to leave our carriage. It was difficult for me with my baby in my arms, but I managed with the assistance of my fellow prisoners. We had arrived in Inta within the Komi Republic far north within the Arctic Circle. Inta was a well known penal colony consisting of several labor camps. We were escorted first to Prison Camp No. 5 where we were quarantined. From there, newly arrived prisoners were sent to one of the other prison camps. I, along with a large number of other prisoners, was assigned to Prison Camp No. 4. Prisoners who were guilty of committing a "political" crime were assigned to Prison Camp No. 4.

All the political prisoners were ordered to form a line at the gate of Prison Camp No. 5. From there the guards were to march us to Prison Camp No. 4. There were many of us, and I was one of several mothers within the group. We were left standing in line exposed to the freezing temperature for several hours. The mothers begged the guards for permission to change the diapers of their babies, but the guards would not permit it. When the mothers became indignant and accused the guards of being cruel and inhumane, the guards reacted by directing their rifles at us and ordering all the mothers to lie down in the snow with their babies.

When we finally arrived at Prison Camp No. 4, most of the babies were suffering from pneumonia. The female doctor at the camp, Milda Yakovlevna, tried to care for the babies professionally but she did not have antibiotics. Using a syringe, she injected the babies with camphor. [Camphor was made by distilling the bark and wood of the camphor tree. It was taken by mouth to help a patient cough up phlegm and it was injected to treat respiratory tract infections. When ingested, camphor could cause serious side effects, even death.] The doctor also bathed each baby with a solution of warm water and mustard. [Mustard seeds contain mustard oil. This antibacterial oil opens up breathing and helps kill germs while it clears congestion in the airways of a human body.] In the end, more than ten of the babies died.

All the "mamkas" in the prison camp were assigned to the same barrack. Each of us was given our own bed which was made up of long wooden planks. The planking was hard and uncomfortable. In time, I filled a large sack with wood shavings and that became my mattress. I used it as a mattress for a long time. The barrack included a "filling room." When it was time to feed a baby, the "mamka" would go to the "filling room" to breast feed her child. One of the nurses at the camp would hand the "mamka" her baby through a special window in the "filling room." The babies in the camp did not live with their mothers. They were cared for by the prison nurses in a special building called the "Children's House." The mothers would see their babies only during feeding time and for two hours every Sunday. The "Children's House" was surrounded with a high fence to prevent the "mamkas" from having contact with their babies except during the allotted times. They could not even see their babies from a distance.

It was cold and dirty within the "filling room" of the barrack. It was dirty because the "mamkas" entered the room wearing their large, wet, dirty boots. Many of them smoked while they were breast feeding their babies. It concerned me and I proposed that the "filling room" be made more sanitary. It was decided that the person who was on duty in the "filling room" [that would be a female inmate] be required to clean the floor and keep the room heated. She was also to make sure that "mamkas" before entering the "filling room" take off their boots and put out their cigarettes. There was to be no smoking in the "filling room." Most of the "mamkas" supported the changes that were instituted. Some "mamkas" resisted the changes. Among them were several genuine criminals who had been moved to our prison camp after they criticized the Communist regime. [By criticizing the government, they had committed a political crime and thus they were re-identified as political prisoners.] Later, the "mamkas" in our barrack were able to acquire a basin and an iron. We began to wash and iron the babies' diapers.

Everyone in our barrack was put to work and the jobs varied. Some women worked at jobs outside the "zone." [The zone was the area that was enclosed by the barbed wire fencing that surrounded the prison camp.] Others were assigned to work at jobs inside the "zone." The job assignments inside the "zone" were less demanding and no one was permitted to work at these jobs for more than six consecutive months. The jobs included working in the kitchen, cleaning the barracks, washing clothes, repairing clothes and distributing bread.

It was my job to supply the women in my barrack with bread. The "mamkas" were required to breast feed their babies early in the morning; they had to be in the "filling room" by 6:00 A.M. At the same time they were to get their portion of bread which would be given to them by me. Some of them didn't get their bread on time. I told them that they must pick up their bread in the morning. If I set the bread aside in order to give it to them later, it would attract flies and begin to spoil. I warned them that if they did not come on time, I would give their portion to others who would appreciate the extra bread, especially those who worked at physical labor outside the "zone."

Not all physical labor outside of the "zone" was productive. Some of the work was designed to keep the prisoners busy and all of it was meant to punish them. [Punishment was one of the reasons why prisoners were brought to a prison labor camp; they were to be punished for the crimes that they had committed.] Work tasks which were designed to keep the prisoners busy included digging a hole, which would be done by one group, and then filling that same hole which would be done by another group. Ordering one group of prisoners to move large stones to a particular area and then later having another group carry the stones to the original site, were two more activities designed to keep prisoners busy. If a prisoner had been unwilling to cooperate with the State during her or his interrogation before she or he was sentenced, a special notation was made by the State's interrogator. The interrogator was notifying the future prison warden that the person should be assigned to do heavy labor, the kind of labor that would cause the prisoner's death before she or he was scheduled to be released from prison.

The guards at Prison Camp No. 4 were usually poorly educated young men who had been drafted into the armed forces. I suspect that they were raised in rural villages and that they had never been to a big city. Following their arrival at the prison camp compound, they discovered very quickly that their position as guards gave them a degree of power and self importance. They liked the feeling, and their salaries were quite good. Yet, they were not required to work very hard. They were certain that we, the prisoners, were "enemies of the people" and believed our punishment was justified. They did not hesitate to punish us. They did not use our names when they addressed us. Every prisoner was given a number which was sewn on the prison clothes and the guards called the prisoners by their numbers. It was degrading. It was one of several practices used by the guards to strip us of our dignity and make us feel less human.

The babies in the prison camp were viewed by the authorities as innocents. They were not prisoners because they had not committed a crime. They were given better quality food and their diapers and clothes were made from good quality cloth. Each piece of cloth was one meter in length. One woman, who was a supply manager in the prison camp, would often steal some of the cloth and use it to make for herself skirts and blouses. She would also use some of the stolen cloth to bribe others. Her name was Veslukhova. During the war, she was a prisoner in a fascist prison camp. She was clever and the fascists made her the leader in one of the barracks. She was corrupt. I believe that once a person commits an act of corruption it is very difficult for that person to stop.

Why were there so many babies in Prison Camp No. 4? Many of the "mamkas" were pregnant before they arrived at the camp. They had been raped by interrogators or by prison guards following their arrest. Newly arrived female prisoners were sent to the bath house shortly upon their arrival in the prison camp. The men running the prison camp, I mean officers who were camp administrators and privileged workers at the camp, would enter the bath house and choose for themselves the women they wanted to use sexually. They became the "masters" of these women. If a woman refused to cooperate, she was taken and pushed "under a truck" and she was gang raped. She would be left an invalid, an invalid in more than one way.

Sometimes female prisoners were raped by male prisoners. In such cases a large group of male prisoners would enter a women's barrack at night after breaking the lock on the door to the barrack. The men would then break the lights within the barrack and rush to the sleeping women yelling "Ride them horses!" Did the guards know about this? They permitted it. The prisoners had paid them to keep quiet. As a consequence, some of the raped women became pregnant and some gave birth to babies that suffered from the effects of syphilis. In Prison Camp No. 4 there were more than ten small children who suffered from syphilis. They were placed in a separate room within the "Children's House." They were unable to stand; they could barely move; they were unable to speak; they could hardly mumble; they had what might be called flippers instead of arms and legs.

There were "mamkas" who hated their children. One of these "mamkas" was a beautiful woman who was a native of Belorussia. After the fascists invaded Belorussia, she worked for them as a waitress. That is why she was arrested after the war. [She was guilty of collaborating with the enemy.] She was interrogated and it was the interrogator [probably a NKVD officer] who raped her. That is why she hated her child. However, most of the "mamkas" in the prison camp loved their children.

Among the prisoners there were several young women from Moscow. They were wives of British pilots. During the war many military personnel from the United States of America, from Great Britain and from France fought as volunteers with the Soviet troops against the fascists. A number of them fell in love with Russian girls and married them. [A large percentage of these girls worked as interpreters.] After the war the foreign volunteers were ordered to return to their native countries. I assume that many of the foreign volunteers took their Russian wives with them. Most, if not all, of the wives that remained in the Soviet Union were arrested and sentenced to prison.

There were also German women within the camp. Following the war against Germany, the victorious Allies divided the occupied nation of Germany into four zones. France, Great Britain, the United States of America and the Soviet Union were each designated a zone and military forces of the occupying countries were stationed in the zones. At the same time, there were German families whose members lived in different zones. If a German woman who lived in the British zone visited her parents who lived in the zone occupied by the Soviet Union, she might be arrested and accused of spying. If it was decided that she was guilty of espionage, she would be identified as a political prisoner and serve her sentence in Prison Camp No. 4.

When a child in our prison camp reached the age of two, it was brought to a State-run orphanage outside of the camp, somewhere in the Komi Republic. A piece of fabric bearing the child's name was wrapped around it's wrist for identification. The "mamka" was permitted to see her child one more time and then it was taken from her arms and sent off. Both mothers and their children would cry as they were forcibly separated from each other. It was terrible. It was so terrible that even the most hardened nurses and the cruelest guards wept. Each separation was a scene out of Hell and I will never forget it. Tears still come to my eyes when I think back to those scenes.

I learned later that there were "mamkas" who lost contact with their babies after they were brought to the State-run orphanage. [At the age of two a child was still called a baby.] The cloth labels bearing the babies' names were taken off their wrists at different times for various reasons and sometimes they were re-attached to the wrong babies. This happened to the baby of a "mamka" in our camp. She was Ukrainian and her parents traveled to the State-run orphanage to bring their grandchild home so that they could raise the child while their daughter was still serving her sentence. Months later, the "mamka's" parents sent their daughter a photograph of the child. The "mamka" noticed immediately that the child was not her son. By the time her parents were notified of the mistake, they had adopted the baby boy. They loved the child and he loved them. Yet, the grandparents had to give him up.

Sofia told the authors that she decided that her baby boy should not remain in the prison labor camp. She was permitted to see him only during the short times when she fed him in the "filling room" and for two hours each Sunday. Her baby was being raised by the nurses in the "Children's House" within the camp. The living conditions within the camp were such that her son had become ill. The freezing temperature outside made it impossible for her baby to be brought outside; he had to remain inside. The parents of Sofia had promised their daughter, after she was imprisoned at "Kresty" prison in Leningrad, that should she be sent to a prison labor camp and if the conditions in the camp were unhealthy, in any way, that they would raise her child, their grandchild. With that in mind, Sofia wrote her parents in Viritza and begged them to take her child and raise him. She had named her son Andrei.

The prisoners in Prison Camp No. 4 were permitted by the authorities to write and send only two letters to relatives or friends in a year. On May 3, 1950, Sofia wrote her parents a letter asking them to take her baby and raise the child in Viritza. She was sure that her parents would take Andrei; they had promised her they would. However, the trip from Viritza to Inta in the Komi Republic and then back to Viritza would be difficult and Sofia did not know if her parents were able to make the long trip.

The authors were given almost all the letters that Sofia wrote while in the prison labor camp and also the letters that she received. They also were given permission to use them. The letter that Sofia wrote to her parents dated May 3, 1950, reads as follows:

May 3, 1950

My dears! I have arrived at the place [of my imprisonment]. My boy was placed in the "Children's House" (a kind of nursery at the prison compound). When we talked [back in "Kresty" prison in Leningrad] we agreed that if the conditions for my baby in the prison labor camp are not good, you will take the baby. I had hoped to keep him here with me until autumn. By that time he will be a year old and it will be easier for you to take care of him. But I believe it is necessary for him to be taken from here as soon as possible or he will die. I understand that raising my son will burden you with additional concerns and responsibilities, but he is precious to me and I want him out of harm's way. He is an excellent child and before we arrived at the prison camp he was healthy and quiet. But now he is ill. He has an abnormally high temperature; the doctors suspect that he is suffering from pneumonia. The weather here is not good; it is unwise to walk outside and the air inside is unhealthy.

I beg of you to take Andrei from here. I know that the trip to the prison camp will be expensive so do not bring me anything. I just want to save my son. I am trying to spend as much time with him as I am allowed. I know that he misses me when I am not with him. He cries when I am not with him. He is fed only my milk. I shall try to feed him solid food in the near future. He now weighs 6.5 kilograms [14 pound and 5 ounces]. The question is - who will come to the prison camp to get my son? Who is able to take care of him on the long journey back to Leningrad? I believe you know to what I am referring, especially mother.

I will be given the opportunity to write my next letter in November. Prisoners are allowed to send only two letters in a year. I desire to see you, but I know that is not possible. I will not be given the opportunity to meet with the person who comes to take Andrei from here.

My address is:

Komi Republic, Kozhvinskiy District, Inta, P.O. box 388/14. Firsova S.

Sofia's brother Pavel and her aunt Lidiya would travel by train to the prison compound in the Komi Republic to get Sofia's son, Andrei. It was a long, difficult trip but brother Pavel was familiar with such trips. As an educated and trained geologist, he had already participated in many faraway expeditions and had worked in the arctic area of the Urals. It was August 1950 when Pavel and Lidiya arrived at Prison Camp No. 4. Andrei was eight months old and Sofia would breast feed him for the last time in the "filling room." Then she said good-bye. The prison camp officers would not permit her to bring Andrei to the "Children's House" where Pavel was waiting to receive her baby boy. Sofia saw Pavel but from a far distance. Tears came to Sofia's eyes as she recalled that scene.

The two letters that follow this paragraph were written by Sofia and were addressed to her parents after her brother Pavel had delivered her baby boy to her parents in Viritza. The two letters are not dated and they are not signed. They were sent illegally from the prison camp compound. The authors were not told how Sofia had been able to accomplish this. In the letters, she expresses her concern for her parents' health, especially her mother's health. She wonders what her husband thinks of his son, Andrei, and what her husband thinks of her. She is confident that her parents will take good care of her child and will love him the way she loves her child. Sofia longs for her baby and she thinks of him at all times. She writes that she tries to imagine his physical features and his various behaviors. She will miss his first steps and will not hear his first words. Yet she knows that sending him away was necessary and having him live with them is wise. She urges her parents to take care of themselves and to believe that she will rejoin them in the future.

Undated Letter One

Your letters cause me great concern. I am especially concerned for mother and her health. She must not despair so much. She must not suffer so much for me. We have to think positive and believe that the future will be much better. Let's hope that I survive this ordeal and hope that I remain healthy. Up to now I am in good health.

Please do not send me any more stuff. We [referring to the detainees in the prison labor camp] do not remain in one location for a long period of time. When we are moved to another area we bring with us only those items that we are able to carry with our hands.

I wonder what the baby's father thinks of his son. I gather from your letters that he is willing to leave Andrei in your care. I believe that this is wise. I do not know what he thinks of me. Give him my best wishes.

I promise you that I will take care of myself and be smart. I will do any job to which I am assigned and I know how to get along with people. I know that you will raise my child with great care, with love and with your love for me. I hope that he will never think badly of me. I want to be with him every day and night. I desire to sing songs to him as he is about to fall asleep. I haven't had the opportunity to do that here. At the prison camp I am a wet nurse and nothing more.

Undated Letter Two

I do not know what the future holds but I believe it will be good. I want you to know that even here [in this prison labor camp] I am happy and it is thinking of my son that makes me happy.

I desire to be with him all the time, to watch him grow and to guide him. I think of him every moment. I try to imagine his eyes, his mischievousness and his laughter. It is a shame that I will not be able to see him take his first steps and that I will not hear his first words. But I know that it is much better for him to be with you. So I must accept my condition which is being alone.

I hope that you understand how important it is for me to know every detail of my son's actions. I know that you will find the time to write me and keep me informed. I do appreciate all of your efforts. I urge you to take care of yourselves and do not despair. You must believe that there will come a time when we will be together again.

In September Sofia addressed her parents with the second letter that the authorities permitted her to send in 1950. By this time, she was working in the "Children's House" within Prison Camp No. 4. She had already made several improvements within the nursery to make it more sanitary. Many of the children (all of them under the age of two) called her "Mamma" which was both wonderful and heartbreaking because whenever they did, she was reminded of her own child who was being raised by her parents. Sofia was happy that Andrei was bringing her parents joy and thankful that they had sent photographs of her son. She wrote that she awakened time and time again each night to look at the photographs. She feared that Andrei would not remember her. Yet, she acknowledged that it had been necessary to get Andrei out of the prison camp. She assured her parents that she was taking good care of herself for them and for her child. She believed that the future promised to be better. The letter reads as follows:

September 26, 1950

My Dears, how are you doing?

I am so happy that I have this opportunity to write you my second letter. I have been anticipating this opportunity for such a long time.

I am in good health. After I stopped breast feeding Andrei, I suffered no more than 4 to 5 days. Generally speaking, my pregnancy went well; I had no difficulties giving birth and I was able to feed Andrei my milk. He ate only my milk because I had no sugar or animal milk to feed him. It must be difficult feeding him manufactured milk [infant formula]. But apparently he is in good health. I am happy that he has brought you joy. I long to be with you and to hug my baby. I appreciate the photographs that you have sent me. For several nights after I received the photographs, I would awaken many times to look again and again at the image of my little swallow [her son Andrei]. I would give half of the world for the opportunity to embrace him and fondle him. Being deprived of this wonderful experience is the worst of all of my misfortunes.

On the other hand, I am very happy that he has been taken out of this place and that he now lives with you. I am not worried about his health. I know that you love him and will protect him. I am sure that you give him the kind of care that a mother would give him.

Oh my God! I am so afraid that he will not remember me. Where can I find the strength to live with the reality of our separation? Initially, I had great difficulty observing a "mamka" breast-feeding her baby. I would almost cry. But I am sure that the decision to get him [Andrei] out of here was wise. It is better for him to be with you and it is better for me as well.

I am the superintendant of the nursery [the "Children's House"] in the camp. The living conditions within the nursery have been improved [because of Sofia's efforts] since my arrival. I am strengthened by the belief that the future promises a better life. I do take care of myself for you and for my child.

My dear mom, I believe that you understand my yearning and my suffering. You understand why it is important for me to know everything about my child: how he sleeps, how he walks, and how he plays. Is he mischievous? I have not seen him walk or play.

Kissing you. Your Sonya [Sonya was another name used by her parents to address their daughter.]

P.S. Putting letters inside parcels is not permitted.

P.P.S. With my son so far away, my feeling of motherhood is buried deep within me. Thus, it gives me no joy. This is understandable for I have never heard him say the word "mommy."

There are a lot of children at the prison camp that call me "Momma Sonya." It is wonderful that other children address me in this way, yet it hurts that I am not called "mommy" by my own child.

I feel like I am stuck on a treadmill. I try to help others as much as possible. Helping others gives me purpose for living.

In early 1951 Sofia finally received a letter from her husband, Nicholas Firsov. The address on the envelope was written in his handwriting but inside Sofia found only a subpoena informing her that her husband had started the proceedings for a divorce. Shortly thereafter, Sofia received a letter from her parents informing her that Nicholas was planning to take Andrei away from them; he was seeking custody of his son. It is believed by the authors that Sofia must have received a second letter from her husband in which he informed her that he was seeking custody of their son.

Sofia responded to all of these developments by addressing her husband with her own letter dated April 1, 1951. The authors have concluded that this letter (Sofia's letter) was never sent to Nicholas. In the letter Sofia tried to reason with Nicholas, the father of her son. She did not understand why he wanted to take Andrei, their son, away from her parents who provided Andrei with love and wonderful care. She felt that if Nicholas was given custody of Andrei, she would in turn lose her son who was so important in her life. She did not believe that she would be giving birth to anymore children. Andrei would be her only child and she did not want to lose him. The letter reads as follows:

April 1, 1951

I am at a loss even now in spite of the fact that a day has gone by since I received your letter (that is if it can be called "a letter"). I cannot imagine what new danger will threaten me and what new trouble awaits me. Oh my God! Maybe I will be able to touch your heart with the words in this letter. Maybe your heart is not completely petrified. Maybe it will respond to the immeasurable pain in my soul. In that case, I will not be sorry that I have used one of the two opportunities the authorities have granted me each year to write a letter.

In the letter I received yesterday, you stated that you have decided to take my child from my parents. I have given your decision much thought and I do not understand your purpose for doing this. You are aware of the conditions that I endured during the second half of my pregnancy. You know that I gave birth to our son in horrendous conditions and you know where I was finally sent. You cannot imagine the price that I paid to survive. I sent my child to my parents knowing that he would be exposed to a wonderful environment. He would be surrounded with love and care. In the letters that I have received from my mother, she describes in great detail the kind of care that my son is receiving. As a result, I feel alive once again.

The most valuable things in life have been taken from me. The birth of Andrei gave me reason to live. And now you are trying to take my purpose for living from me. God forbid that you take my child from my parents; if that should happen then my life will lose its meaning. In my current condition, Andrei is everything to me. I dream about my future meeting with him. The letters that describe him and the photographs that my parents have sent, bring joy to my life.

I am happy that you have paternalistic feelings. It is good that a child, who is deprived of his mother, has a father. But why are you trying to take Andrei from my parents? I do not know of a better environment for Andrei. He is my only child and it is obvious that I will not give birth to any more children. When my parents lost me, they were given Andrei, their grandson, who has brought joy into their lives. They write me often and in great detail about Andrei because they know how important it is for me. I know that there have been many times when Andrei was brought to your place and that you spent time together, but I have not received one word from you about your visits with him. My parents cultivate in Andrei's soul a love for me. You are young and unmarried and have the opportunity to be a husband to someone else and be a father again. In fact, you may even have several children. Why are you trying to kill me and my parents?

Oh my Sunny! If you knew what grief your father has caused, you would run away from him and back to your granny. Think about this, why is it necessary for Andrei to live with you? Your mother is old and cannot take care of him. Your Aunt Vera is too busy with her job. You will have to take Andrei to a nursery and then he will be raised by a stranger. On the other hand, Andrei is my parent's grandson and even more he is a part of me.

I think that in your present situation you will soon have a new mother-in-law. Is it possible that we can get through this?

You don't have to deprive me of all my happiness. I am suffering as it is. You don't have to remove the ground from under me. If I should be deprived of my son then I will not continue my miserable existence.

[Andrei's] Mother

Sofia will also write her Uncle Arkadiy about her former husband's actions. She will write him several letters. One is not dated and a second one is dated July 10, 1952. The authors suspect that the letters were sent out of the prison camp compound under someone else's name. A prisoner who had no friends or relatives or who did not want to contact them would allow another prisoner to use the two letters that she was allotted each year. This might be done for a payment or for a favor. This is probably how Sofia was able to send several letters to her uncle.

The undated letter to Uncle Arkadiy reads as follows:

How can I go on living? Where can I find the strength to do so? I am trying to stay focused. I am living in hope.

I appear to be defenseless against the brazenness [of my former husband]. I do not know what chance I have against Nicholas in this animalistic struggle for survival. Because of this struggle, I have become ancient and exhausted. I feel as if I am a thousand years old. I don't mean just my physical appearance, but in my soul and my mind as well. Recently, I looked at myself in a mirror and was shocked at the deadness of my eyes. I do not want to return home an old woman.

Do not think that I am discouraged or that I bear a grudge against all mankind? On the contrary, I sympathize with people even those who are the source of my suffering.

My parents have kept silent about my former husband. But I can guess, and it does not improve my state of mind. I am concerned about my child. I am afraid that my former husband will try to take my son from my parents. I hope that they will not permit that to happen.

I shall never have another child as nice as my little boy. Every day, early in the morning and in the evening, I take out my photographs of him and look at his pretty face. I think often of his small delicate body, his arms and legs and his wonderful eyes. Will he recognize me when we are reunited? I will be such a dedicated mother if fate permits me to be reunited with him. It was you who predicted that I would become a mother of three children. I have dreams in which I am the mother of three children.

You promised that you would send a package of books. I appreciate it. Books and magazines are highly valued in the prison camp.

Send my love and kisses to my parents and to my son about whom I think twenty-four hours a day.

The second letter that Sofia sent to her Uncle Arkadiy reads as follows:

July 10, 1952

I am sending the letter that I addressed to Nicholas. I am faced with a serious problem. I received a letter from mother; she reported that she is not satisfied with Andrei's behavior. He is spoiled and rude. No doubt, it is due to the influence that his father's family has had on him. As he grows older, that influence will become stronger. I am in a panic. Andrei has lived the last six months with his father's family and I am sure he [Andrei] has completely forgotten me. Nobody in that family will talk to Andrei about me. It concerns me and I wrote Nicholas about my concern. It is not my first letter to him. I wrote a year and a half ago, but he did not reply. I do not expect him to reply to this letter either. If he does, I hope he is straight forward and honest. I hate hypocrisy.

On November 26, Sofia wrote the second letter of the two she was permitted to write in 1952. The letter was addressed to her parents in Viritza. Her son Andrei had turned three years old and she longed to be with him. Time was moving on and Sofia was unable to experience the joy of seeing her little boy mature and grow. It was painful for her and caused her to feel melancholy. The letter reads as follows:

November 26, 1952

My dear [parents]!

Yesterday I thought about you all day long. The time passes by so quickly. Andrei is already three years old. My little chick is already good-sized. Silently, I talk to him. I want him to know me. Will that ever come true?

I am waiting for your detailed description of his birthday. Was it nice? What is his character? I dream that one day I will be able to hold him in my arms, to play games with him and to just enjoy his presence. Oh my God! I would be so happy. I desire to stand by his bed and sing a lullaby as he falls asleep. I have dreamed of being with my son and singing songs to him for such a long time. Year after year passes and the opportunity to be with my child decreases. I feel that I will never become a part of his childhood experiences; he will live his childhood without a mother. The place in his heart that is set aside for me will be overgrown with weeds because I am being deprived of the opportunity to plant seeds of love there. It is a most severe punishment and the pain in my heart will never leave. I can imagine how he will react when he sees me for the first time. He will see a decrepit ruin and I am afraid he will disdainfully turn away from me. The thought of that happening causes me to feel sad and depressed. Nevertheless, I promise that I will work at maintaining a cheerful spirit.

Joseph Stalin died on March 5, 1953. His death was announced to the Soviet citizens and more than one million viewed his embalmed body in Moscow before it was laid to rest on March 9, 1953, in Lenin's Mausoleum. The death of Stalin came as a shock to most Soviet citizens. He had ruled the Soviet Union since the 1920s and had led the Soviet Union to a military victory during the Great Patriotic War. Many citizens wondered what would happen to the Soviet Union now that Stalin was gone; many were deeply concerned. Sofia and the other prisoners in Prison Camp No. 4 manifested a different response. When they learned about Stalin's death, they were relieved and happy. However, they made sure that they did not express their sentiments for fear that they would be punished with solitary confinement.

Following Stalin's death, the regulations at the prison labor camp were modified and became more relaxed. The prisoners were permitted to sing songs, recite poetry and participate in interesting conversations. Some prisoners began drawing pictures and embroidering. The prisoners were also permitted to address one letter per month to family members or friends outside of the prison compound. In September 1953, (by this time Stalin had been dead for seven months) Sofia wrote her parents and informed them of the good news. The letter reads as follows:

September 13, 1953

My dear [parents],

As you must have already noticed, prisoners have been given permission to send out a letter every month. It is a wonderful development. I am happy that Andrei will be spending one more month with you. At the end of the month, please send Andrei to a kindergarten [child day care center]. This will be good for him. It will help him grow and mature. I should also like for him to study music because it helps develop a person's softer and more delicate nature.

Mom, I have cared for many children at the prison camp. I am emotionally tied to them. They call me "Mommy Sonya." It is a great compliment. It means that they appreciate all that I have done for them. Recently some of them [those who turned two years old] were released from the "Children's House" in the camp and were sent to a State-run orphanage. Please do not get rid of Andrei's toys and children's books. Later [after Andrei has outgrown the toys and books] I would like for you to send them to the children at the State-run orphanage with the following inscription: "From Mommy Sonya." Maybe it will also be possible to send them apples. While in the prison camp, they were never given an apple.

In the letter above Sofia refers to her work in the "Children's House" in Prison Camp No. 4. In fact, during Sofia's time at the prison camp she worked in the prison nursery for three consecutive work periods, eighteen consecutive months. This was unusual. According to the work policy enforced at the prison camp, a prisoner who was assigned to a job inside the prison "zone" was to work at that job for only six months and then she or he was reassigned to another job, one that was outside of the "zone."

Jobs inside the "zone" were usually set aside for camp informers. The camp informers, Sofia discovered, were usually concerned more about their own welfare than the welfare of others. Sofia observed this attitude while working in the nursery, the "Children's House." The prisoners who worked with her in the nursery would steal food and medicines that were meant for the babies. Sofia was shocked when she saw this taking place. Sofia was also concerned about the unsanitary conditions that existed in the "Children's House." Through the efforts of Sofia, the nursery was made more sanitary. Sofia's efforts were appreciated by the "mamkas" and most likely by the prison camp directors.

In 1954 Sofia received from her mother two short letters, one bearing bad news and the other bearing good news. In the first, dated June 22, 1954, Sofia's mother informed her daughter that Andrei's father had already told them (Sofia's parents) that he would not permit Andrei to spend the summer vacation with them. Nicholas would not tell them where Andrei would be living during the vacation. The letter reads as follows:

June 22, 1954

Dear Sonya,

You are already aware that Nicholas' parents will not permit Andrei to spend the summer vacation with us. [The decision may have been made by Nicholas' parents or Nicholas may have decided this alone or the three together may have made the decision.] Nicholas would not even tell us where Andrei is staying this summer. I suspect that he does not want Andrei to get to know his mother [through Sofia's parents].

The second short letter, this one bearing good news, was sent on July 8, 1954. The first part of the letter was written by Sofia's mother and the second was penned by Sofia's friend, Lialia Fishman. Lialia's husband had earlier been arrested by the State and sent to a prison labor camp. Lialia informed Sofia that her husband's prison sentence had been commuted and that he would be returning home to Leningrad within the near future. Lialia wrote that she was sure that this would happen to Sofia as well and that soon they would be together in Leningrad. The letter reads as follows:

July 8, 1954

Dear Sonya,

Each time, when I harvest strawberries, I break down and cry because Andrei and you are not here with me.

[The next paragraph in the letter was written by Lialia Fishman.]

Dear Sonya,

Your mother is visiting me and I am taking this opportunity to share with you some excellent news. My husband has been granted amnesty and he has been released from the prison labor camp where he was being held. He will soon return home. I am sure that very soon you will be released as well and we shall be together again. I am kissing you and am waiting for you. Your friend, Lialia.

Chapter Eight

Sofia's Release from Prison

Sofia's prison sentence was commuted and she was released from prison in October 1954. She was told the good news by the prison camp's warden after she was brought into his office. "It is a pity," he announced, "but you are to be set free." He was sorry to see Sofia leave because she had been such a positive influence in Prison Camp No. 4. Upon hearing the warden's announcement, Sofia's legs buckled underneath her.

Several days later, Sofia was in Leningrad where her mother met her. Sofia was thinking about her son, Andrei, who she had not seen since her brother Pavel had taken her eight month baby from the prison labor camp. He was now six years old.

On the second day after Sofia's arrival in Leningrad, she and her mother went to see Andrei. He lived with his father in the same apartment on Marata Prospect where Sofia had been arrested back in 1949. As they made their way to Marata Prospect, Sofia thought back to the many times, in the prison camp, when she tried to imagine what her first meeting with Andrei would be like. Would he recognize her?

It was Nicholas who opened the door to the apartment and there was a look of nervousness on his face. Sofia rushed into the apartment and saw Andrei lying on his bed. He was ill. He was thin and pale. "Look," Sofia's mother announced, "it is your mommy, she has returned." "Mom," Andrei asked, "will you ever go away again?" "Never," Sofia promised.

Figure 8.1. Sofia Prupis shortly after her release from the prison labor camp. Courtesy of Alexey Vinogradov.

Afterword

Urkho Rhukanen would be reunited with his wife, Lilya, and sons in Dzezhinskoye where Lilya was working as a teacher. A while later, Urkho and Lilya received a newspaper published in Karelia (politically Karelia was the Karelo-Finnish Soviet Socialist Republic). From the newspaper Urkho and Lilya learned that their former teacher, Mr. Belyayev, had become the Minister of Education in the Soviet republic. They wrote Mr. Belyayev and inquired if there were vacant teaching positions within the republic. Their former teacher replied that there were and he would like for them both to come work for him. Urkho and Lilya and their sons moved to Karelia and settled in Petrozavodsk.

In 1947 Urkho became the director (headmaster, supervisor) of one of the schools in Petrozavodsk and he would remain its director until 1961. In 1956 Urkho was declared completely" rehabilitated" by the State and was readmitted in the Union of Soviet Writers. Urkho had been expelled from this union back in 1937.

Sofia Prupis faced some major difficulties after she returned to Leningrad following her release from the prison labor camp in Inta. Though she had a doctor's degree, she was unable to secure a teaching position. In 1955, Sofia filed a petition for "rehabilitation." She also met an old acquaintance, a graduate from Leningrad State University, and the two got married.

In 1956, the Leningrad city court "rehabilitated" Sofia. Thereafter, she acquired a job teaching at the Leningrad Institute of Electrical Engineering and Communication. Four years later, she defended her second doctoral dissertation and in 1972 she became a full-time professor within the School of Economic Relations at the Leningrad Institute of Electrical Engineering and Communication. As an educator, she would author more than sixty scientific articles and a textbook.

Sofia's son, Andrei, earned a doctor's degree in technical sciences and worked as a professor at the Leningrad State Polytechnical University.

Appendix

POLITICAL ZIONISM

In the nineteenth and twentieth centuries many European Jews responded to anti-Semitism with what became known as political Zionism. They wanted to establish a Jewish homeland in any available territory, not necessarily in Palestine, through cooperation with the European powers. They believed the European powers would support a Jewish national existence outside of Europe because it would rid them of their Jewish problem. The Zionists believed that Jews throughout the world would want to emigrate to the new Jewish political entity which was to be a secular nation.

The first Jew to articulate a political Zionist platform was a Russian physician residing in Odessa. A year after the 1881 pogroms, Leo Pinsker wrote in a pamphlet titled *Auto-Emancipation* that anti-Semitism was a modern phenomenon, beyond the reach of any future triumphs of "humanity and enlightenment." Therefore, Jews must organize themselves to find their own national home wherever possible, not necessarily in their ancestral home in Palestine (the Holy Land).

Pinsker's work attracted the attention of Hibbat Tziyyou (Lovers of Zion), an organization devoted to Hebrew education and national revival. The members of Hibbat Tziyyou took up Pinsker's call for a territorial solution to the Jewish problem. Pinsker, who became the leader of the movement, obtained support from the wealthy Jewish philanthropist, Baron Edmond de Rothschild, who was a Zionist. The funds were to be used to support Jewish agricultural settlements in Palestine at Rishon LeZiyyou, south of Tel Aviv and at Zikhvou Yaaqov, south of Haifa. Although the number of Jews who immigrated to Palestine were small (only some 10,000 settlers by 1891), the immigration was important because it established a Jewish bridgehead in Palestine.

The impetus to founding a Zionist organization with specific goals was provided by Theodor Herzl. Born in Budapest on May 2, 1860, Herzl was educated in Vienna as a lawyer but became a journalist and a playwright. While working in Paris as a correspondent for a Viennese newspaper, Herzl became aware of the pervasiveness of anti-Semitism in French society.

The turning point in Herzl's thinking on the Jewish question occurred during the 1894 Paris trial of Alfred Dreyfus, a Jewish military officer within the French General Staff. He was accused of selling military secrets to Germany. Dreyfus was convicted and sentenced to life in prison. Although he was eventually exonerated, his career was ruined. The trial of Dreyfus and later his exoneration unleashed widespread anti-Semitic demonstrations and riots in France. The Dreyfus affair proved for Herzl that Jews would always be an alien element in the societies in which they resided. It was necessary for Jews to have their own state. He believed that even if they assimilated, Jews would continue to be treated as outsiders.

Herzl put forth his solution to the Jewish problem in a book titled *Der Judenstaat* (*The Jewish State*) published in 1896. He called for the establishment of a Jewish state in any available territory to which the majority of European Jewry would emigrate. He argued that Jews are a nation like all other nations which is why a sovereign state was a solution to their problem. He was convinced that the nations of Europe would grant Jews sovereignty over a portion of land. This solution, he argued, would satisfy both the Zionists and Europe's anti-Semites.

Herzl, in the following selection of excerpts taken from *The Jewish State*, points to the existence of anti-Semitism in countries where Jews "live in perceptible numbers" and he proposes a solution to the "Jewish problem":

> "I do not intend to arouse sympathetic emotions on our behalf. That would be a foolish, futile, and undignified proceeding. I shall content myself with putting the following question to the Jews: Is it not true that, in countries where we live in perceptible numbers, the position of Jewish lawyers, doctors, technicians, teachers, and employees of all descriptions becomes daily more intolerable? Is it not true, that the Jewish middle classes are seriously threatened? Is it not true, that the passions of the mob are incited against our wealthy people? Is it not true, that our poor endure greater sufferings than any other proletariat? I think that this external pressure makes itself felt everywhere. In our economically upper classes it causes discomfort, in our middle classes continual and grave anxieties, in our lower classes absolute despair.
>
> "Everything tends, in fact, to one and the same conclusion, which is clearly enunciated in that classic Berlin phrase: 'Juden 'raus!' (Out with the Jews!)
>
> "I shall now put the Jewish Question in the curtest possible form: Are we to 'get out' now and where to?

"Or, may we yet remain? And, how long?

"Let us first settle the point of staying where we are. Can we hope for better days, can we possess our souls in patience, can we wait in pious resignation till the princes and peoples of this earth are more mercifully disposed towards us? I say that we cannot hope for a change in the current of feeling. And why not? Were we as near to the hearts of princes as are their other subjects, even so they could not protect us. They would only feed popular hatred of Jews by showing us too much favor. By too much, I really mean less than is claimed as a right by every ordinary citizen, or by every race. The nations in whose midst Jews live are all, either covertly or openly, Anti-Semitic. [1]

"The whole plan is in its essence perfectly simple, as it must necessarily be if it is to come within the comprehension of all.

"Let the sovereignty be granted us over a portion of the globe large enough to satisfy the rightful requirements of a nation; the rest we shall manage for ourselves.

"The creation of a new State is neither ridiculous nor impossible. [2]

"Palestine is our ever-memorable historic home. The very name of Palestine would attract our people with a force of marvelous potency." [3]

Herzl actively sought international recognition and the cooperation of the European powers in creating a Jewish state. He preferred that Palestine would become the site for the future Jewish state; however, another site in another area of the world would also be acceptable. In 1903, the year before his death, Herzl met with Kaiser Wilhelm II of German in the hope of obtaining his help. When Herzl failed to secure the Kaiser's assistance, he spent $50,000 in bribes to get an appointment with the sultan of Turkey. However, he quickly discovered that he was not going to succeed with the sultan. So he turned to England. The British foreign office offered 6,000 square miles of uninhabited land in Uganda for a Jewish settlement under the British flag. Herzl accepted the offer and brought the proposal to the sixth world Zionist Congress that was convened in 1903. A bitter battle ensued between Herzl and the Eastern European Zionists. The latter wanted to establish a Jewish state in Palestine, not Uganda. Herzl won by a few votes but died shortly thereafter. Following Herzl's death, the British government withdrew its offer in Uganda.

The Eastern European Jews identified Zionism with Mount Zion located in the city of Jerusalem. Mount Zion was originally the site of an ancient Jebusite fortress in the city of Jerusalem. After David, the second king of Israel, captured the fortress, Jerusalem became a possession. The royal palace was built in Jerusalem and the city became the seat of power in the Kingdom of Israel. The highest part of Jerusalem was the Eastern Hill and the hill became the site of a temple built for the worship of Jehovah God by

Solomon, King David's son and the third king of Israel. The "Mount Zion" mentioned in the book of Isaiah, an ancient Hebrew prophet, and in the book of Psalms seems to refer to the top of the Eastern Hill, generally known as the Temple Mount. In 586 B.C. King Nebuchadnezzar II and his Chaldeans destroyed the city of Jerusalem. A long period of rebuilding followed which included the reconstruction of the Holy Temple on the Eastern Hill, the Temple Mount. In 70 A.D. the city of Jerusalem and the second Holy Temple were destroyed by the Romans. Since that time Jews throughout the world used the name Zion to refer to the Eastern Hill, Mount Zion, and the site of the first and second Holy Temple. It was the most holy place in the world for Jews. It was seen as the connection between God and humanity. In 135 A.D. the Roman Emperor Hadrian rebuilt Jerusalem as a Roman city and named it Aelia Capitolina but the Holy Temple was not rebuilt. Thereafter, whenever Jews used the name Zion it referred to the city of Jerusalem.

The insistence of Eastern European Jews on Palestine as the Jewish homeland remained the focus of the Zionist movement. The failure of the Russian Revolution of 1905 and the wave of pogroms and repressions that followed caused a growing number of Russian Jewish youth to emigrate to Palestine as pioneer settlers. By 1914 there were about 90,000 Jews in Palestine; 13,000 settlers lived in 43 Jewish agricultural settlements. Many of them were supported by the French Jewish philanthropist Baron Edmond de Rothschild. Meanwhile, Arab opposition to the increasing number of Jews in Palestine had grown. Actual conflicts flared up because the Zionists purchased large tracts of land from Arab landowners and subsequently evicted the Arab tenant farmers. The feeling grew among the Arabs that the Zionists had arrived in Palestine to dispossess them of their land.

Following World War One, Palestine came under British rule. Even before the British conquered Palestine from the Ottoman Turkish Empire during the war, the British promised Zionists that they would support the creation of a Jewish national home in Palestine. The promise was documented in the Balfour Declaration which was issued on November 2, 1917. The Declaration was later incorporated into the Mandate for Palestine granted to Great Britain by the Council of the League of Nations on July 24, 1922. The Mandate agreement required Great Britain to prepare the necessary conditions to secure the establishment of a Jewish national home. The Arab population in Palestine responded to these developments with a series of uprisings. They feared that Palestine would eventually become a Jewish state. They were appalled at the prospect of living in a country dominated by Jews. They bitterly resisted Zionism and the British policies that supported it.

Arab uprisings in Palestine led Great Britain to reassess its policies. The British issued the Passfield White Paper which proposed limiting Jewish immigration to Palestine. The Passfield White Paper was quietly withdrawn under pressure coming from Zionists, from British public opinion and from the League of Nations. However, the British eventually did impose severe restrictions on Jewish immigration when they issued the White Paper of 1939. The new restrictions were violently opposed by Zionist underground groups such as the Stern Gang and the Irgun Zrai Lenmi, which committed acts of terrorism and assassinations against the British. They also organized illegal Jewish immigration to Palestine.

The large-scale extermination of European Jews by Adolf Hitler's National Socialists led many Jews to seek refuge in Palestine. But the British would not permit the Jewish refugees to enter Palestine. Rickety boats full of refugees tried to reach Palestine. Many of the boats sank or were caught by the British and turned back or directed to Mauritius or other destinations of internment. In December 1940, a large ship named the S.S. Bulgaria was docked in Haifa with 350 Jewish refugees; it was ordered to return to Bulgaria. The ship capsized in the Turkish straits and 280 people died. A ship named the Struma left Constanta in Rumania with about 769 refugees and reached Istanbul on December 16, 1941. There it was forced to undergo repairs of its engines and leaking hull. The Turks would not grant the refugees sanctuary. The British would not approve transshipment to Mauritius or entry to Palestine. On February 24, 1942, the Turks ordered the Struma out of the harbor. It sank with the loss of 426 men, 269 women and 70 children. Apparently, it had been torpedoed by a Soviet submarine, either because it was mistaken for a German ship or because the Soviets had agreed to collaborate with the British in barring Jewish immigration. Despite the desperate need to find a haven for Jewish refugees during World War Two, the doors of Palestine remained closed to Jewish immigration.

Following World War Two, Great Britain continued to limit Jewish immigration to Palestine. Various Zionist factions united and conducted an underground war against the British. They also applied pressure on the British through the United States. The large-scale extermination of Jews during the war had caused many people in the United States to embrace Zionism. The British responded by submitting the Palestine problem to the newly formed United Nations.

In September 1947, representatives to the United Nations Special Committee on Palestine (UNSCOP) made far-reaching recommendations for the partition of Palestine into two independent states. The Jewish state was to include Eastern Galilee, the coastal strip along the Mediterranean Sea (excluding Jaffa and the coastal strip down to Gaza) and the Negev. The Palestinian Arab state was to include Upper and Western Galilee, the West Bank and the Gaza Strip. The city of Jerusalem and its environs were to be an international enclave to be used by the citizens of both states. The Palestinian Arabs did not accept the partition plan. The Zionists did. On November 29, 1947, the United Nations' General Assembly ratified the recommendations made by UNSCOP and on May 14, 1948, David Ben-Gurion announced the founding of the State of Israel. Fifty-one years earlier, in 1897, Herzl had declared at the first world Zionist Congress held in Basel that in fifty years the world would recognize a Jewish state.

LEON TROTSKY AND TROTSKYISM

At the dawn of the twentieth century, Russia was a politically authoritarian and economically backward empire. The Romanov dynasty headed by Tsar Nicholas II regarded itself as a divine right monarchy, ruling with the help of a large bureaucracy and an army that was used toward territorial conquest and against rebellious subjects. A secret police that had made Siberia notorious as the site for Russian penal colonies kept down dissent, but opposition against autocracy could not be quieted. Liberals, desiring to bring about political, social and economic reforms through peaceful and legal avenues, and revolutionaries, using terrorism, sought to overthrow autocracy. The revolutionaries looked mostly to the Russian peasantry as well as Russia's industrial workers to help bring about the fall of Russia's autocracy.

The people of imperial Russia faced major problems in the latter years of the nineteenth century. The peasant population had increased by more than fifty percent between 1861 and 1900, due mostly to a high birth rate and a declining death rate. The increase in the peasant population meant a reduction in individual peasant land holdings. At the same time, Russia experienced the growth of a large-scale machine industry, which resulted in the emergence of a small, urban working class. Since industrialization was new to Russia, its workers labored under working conditions that were both unsafe and unhealthy. Wages were low; the average workday in a mill was from twelve to fourteen hours. The poor treatment from which the workers suffered, filled within them a feeling of deep discontent and militant consciousness.

It was Leon Trotsky who, along with others, would bring political revolution to the Russian Empire. Trotsky was born Leon Davidovich Bronstein on November 7, 1879 in the village of Yanovka in the Kherson Province of Ukraine, then part of the Russian Empire. He was the fifth of eight children of a Jewish farmer, David Leontievich Bronstein and his wife Anna Bronstein. Although the family was ethnically Jewish, it was not religious, and the languages spoken at home were Russian and Ukrainian instead of Yiddish.

When Trotsky was about ten years old, his father sent him to school in Odessa. Six years later, in 1896, he was transferred to Nikolaev where he became involved in revolutionary activities. Trotsky was first a Narodnik, a Russian agrarian socialist, but he gradually shifted towards Marxism. Instead of pursuing a degree in mathematics, Trotsky helped organize, in early 1897 in Nikolaev, the first illegal workers' organization, the South Russian Workers' Union. Using the name Lvov, Trotsky wrote and printed leaflets and proclamations, distributed revolutionary pamphlets and popularized socialist ideas among industrial workers and revolutionary students.

In January 1898, Trotsky and more than 200 members of the South Russian Workers' Union were arrested. Trotsky would spend the next two and a half years in various prisons awaiting trial. Two months after his arrest and imprisonment, the First Congress of the newly formed Russian Social Democratic Labor Party was held. From that point on, Trotsky affiliated himself with that party. While in prison, Trotsky married a fellow Marxist, Alexandra Sokolovskaya, and studied philosophy. In 1900 Trotsky was sentenced to four years in exile in Siberia, where his two daughters, Nina and Zen, were born.

It was in Siberia that Trotsky became aware of disagreements within the Russian Social Democratic Labor Party. Some Social Democrats known as "economists" argued that the party should concentrate on helping industrial workers gain a better standard of living. Others argued that overthrowing the monarchy was more important and that a well-organized and disciplined revolutionary party was essential. Trotsky sided with the latter opinion.

Trotsky escaped from Siberia in the summer of 1902, with a forged passport bearing the name Leon Trotsky, which he adopted as his primary revolutionary pseudonym. He later said that the name Trotsky was that of a prison guard in Odessa. His wife remained behind in Siberia and their separation became permanent.

Trotsky made his way to London, where he joined Georgi Plekhanov, Julius Martov and other Russian Social Democrats who were working with Vladimir Lenin on a revolutionary newspaper entitled *Iskra* (*The Spark*). Despite various obstacles, Lenin and his comrades managed to smuggle *Iskra* into Russia clandestinely, where it made an enormous impact. Lenin welcomed Trotsky and under the pen name Pero (feather or pen in Russian) Trotsky soon became one of the paper's leading writers.

The six editors of *Iskra* were evenly split between the "old guard" led by Plekhanov and the "new guard" led by Lenin and Martov. Not only were Plekhanov's supporters older (in their 40s and 50s), but they had spent the previous 20 years in European exile together. Members of the "new guard" were in their early 30s and had only recently come from Russia. Lenin, who was trying to establish a permanent majority against Plekhanov within *Iskra*, expected Trotsky, then 23 years old, to side with the "new guard." Lenin wrote in March 1903:

"I suggest to all the members of the editorial board that they co-optate 'Pero' as a member of the board on the same basis as other members. [. . .] We very much need a seventh member, both as a convenience in voting (six being an even number), and as an addition to our forces. 'Pero' has been contributing to every issue for several months now; he works in general most energetically for the *Iskra*; he gives lectures (in which he has been very successful). In the section of articles and notes on the events of the day, he will not only be very useful, but absolutely necessary. Unquestionably a man of rare abilities, he has conviction and energy, and he will go much further."[4]

Plekhanov vetoed the proposal. He believed, that Trotsky would support the "new guard" and Lenin and that would place the "old guard" in a minority. Consequently, Trotsky did not become a full member of the editorial board; however, he would participate in its meetings in an advisory capacity.

In late 1902, Trotsky met Natalia Sedova, who soon became his companion and, from 1903 until his death, his wife. They had two children together, Leon Sedova and Sergey Sedova. Trotsky and his first wife, Alexandra Sokolovskaya, continued to maintain a friendly relationship until Alexandra disappeared in 1937 during Josef Stalin's Great Purges.

At the Second Congress of the Russian Social Democratic Labor Party, convened by *Iskra* and held in London in 1903, there emerged a dispute between Lenin and Julius Martov. Lenin and his supporters argued for a small party of professional revolutionaries with a large fringe of non-party sympathizers and supporters. Martov and his supporters argued for a larger and less disciplined party. Martov won the vote 28 to 23 but Lenin was unwilling to accept the result and formed a faction known as the Bolsheviks. Those who remained loyal to Martov became known as Mensheviks. Trotsky and most of the *Iskra* editors supported Martov but in September 1904 Trotsky left the Mensheviks. From that point until 1917, Trotsky remained a self-described "non-factional Social Democrat." During that time, Trotsky would try to reconcile the different groups within the party and as a result Trotsky would sometimes disagree with Lenin and other prominent party members.

The year 1904 was difficult for the Russian workers. The prices of essential goods rose and real wages declined. In St. Petersburg, Russia's capital city, a Russian Orthodox priest named Father Gapon, hoping to deflect the workers from revolutionary ideas, urged the workers to petition Tsar Nicholas II to establish an eight-hour workday and better working conditions, to grant them civil liberties and to convene a constituent assembly.

On Sunday morning, January 9, 1905, Father Gapon led a group of industrial workers from various parts of the city toward the Winter Palace, the home of the tsar and his family in St. Petersburg. The marchers carried icons and portraits of the tsar, and they sang patriotic hymns, including "God Save the Tsar." As the petitioners approached the Winter Palace, they were ordered to halt. They disregarded the order and so the commander of the tsar's troops ordered his men to fire on the peaceful demonstrators. More than one hundred people were killed, and many more were wounded.

The news of Bloody Sunday, as it became known, undermined the people's faith in the tsar and united them against autocracy. Throughout the empire the massacre caused an angry uproar culminating in labor unrest, peasant insurrections, student demonstrations and mutinies in both the army and navy. Peasants, organizing themselves at the village level, discussed seizing the property of their landlords. Urban workers joined together in organizations that called for a general strike and the people who participated in the strike demanded a democratic republic, the release of political prisoners and the disarming of the government police. Most business and government offices were closed, and Russia's economic life came to a halt.

The tsarist government managed to restore order in the fall of 1905 after agreeing to institute political reforms. In October, Tsar Nicholas II issued a manifesto that promised full civil liberties, a constitution and the creation of the Duma—an elected legislature with the power to enact laws. The October Manifesto was supposed to transform autocratic Russia into a constitutional monarchy. The constitution, which went into effect in 1906, stated that for a measure to become a law it had to be passed by the delegates in both houses of the Duma; however, the tsar retained absolute veto power. The tsar would also determine the duration of the Duma's sessions, and he had the right to dissolve it at will if he set a date for new elections. Article 87 within the constitution allowed the executive (the tsar) to rule by decree. After the revolutionary crisis had passed, the tsarist government returned to its reactionary ways and restricted the authority of the Duma.

After the events of Bloody Sunday, Trotsky secretly returned to the Russian Empire in February 1905. At first he wrote leaflets for an underground printing press in Kiev, but soon he moved to the capital city, St. Petersburg. There he worked with both the Bolsheviks as well as the local Mensheviks. A secret police agent, however, betrayed Trotsky and in May he fled to rural Finland.

Shortly before Trotsky's return to the capital city, the Mensheviks organized an elected non-party revolutionary organization representing the workers in St. Petersburg. It was called the St. Petersburg Soviet of Workers' Deputies. It was the first soviet of workers. (Soviets were councils consisting of deputies representing the people who elected them.) Following the example of the St. Petersburg Soviet, many other soviets were organized in the next few months. Overwhelmingly, they were in cities, but several also appeared among peasants and soldiers.

At the time of Trotsky's arrival in the capital city, the St. Petersburg Soviet of Workers' Deputies was led by Khrustalyov-Nosav (Georgi Nosav, alias Pyotr Krustalyov) as its chairman. Trotsky joined the St. Petersburg Soviet under the name "Yanovsky" (after the village Yanovka where he was born) and was elected vice-chairman. Most of the manifestos and resolutions of the Soviet were the work of Trotsky, who also edited its journal *Izvestia* (*The News*). After Khrustalyov-Nosav's arrest on November 26, 1905, Trotsky was elected chairman of the St. Petersburg Soviet.

On December 2, 1905, the St. Petersburg Soviet called upon the people to withhold their taxes. The government responded by arresting and jailing about half of the more than 500 Soviet members including Trotsky. He and other Soviet leaders were put on trial in 1906 on charges of supporting an armed rebellion. At the trial, Trotsky delivered some of the best speeches of his life. Nevertheless, he was convicted and sentenced, in October 1906, to exile in Siberia for life.

While in prison, awaiting his trial, Trotsky wrote *Permanent Revolution: Results and Prospects.* In the book he developed what became known as the theory of permanent revolution. Trotsky argued that it would be impossible to create a socialist society in Russia in isolation from the rest of Europe. He believed that a Russian socialist state would be faced with the pressures of a hostile capitalist world and it would survive only if socialist revolutions quickly succeeded in other countries as well. Thus, socialist revolutions needed to be fostered worldwide. It was Trotsky's hope that an example in Russia would inspire socialists in other countries: "We rest all our hope on the possibility that our revolution will unleash the European revolution. If the insurrectionary peoples of Europe do not crush imperialism, then we shall be crushed—that is indubitable. Either the Russian revolution will raise the whirlwind of struggle in the West, or the capitalists of all countries will crush our revolution."[5]

In January 1907, Trotsky escaped en route to exile and made his way, eventually, to Vienna, Austria. It was in Vienna, that Trotsky became close to Adolph Joffe, his friend for the next twenty years. In October 1908, he started a bi-weekly Russian language Social Democratic paper aimed at Russian workers. It was called *Pravda* (*The Truth*) and was co-edited by Trotsky and Joffe and others and was smuggled into Russia. The paper avoided factional politics and proved popular with Russian industrial workers.

When various Bolshevik and Menshevik factions tried to re-unite at the January 1910 Central Committee meeting of the Russian Social Democratic Labor Party held in Paris, Trotsky's *Pravda* was made a party-financed central organ. This was done over Lenin's objections. Lev Kamenev, Trotsky's brother-in-law, was added to the editorial board from the Bolsheviks, but the unification attempts failed and in August 1910 Kamenev resigned from the board. Trotsky continued publishing *Pravda* for another two years until it finally folded in April 1912.

When the Bolsheviks started a new workers-oriented newspaper in St. Petersburg on April 22, 1913, they called it *Pravda* as well. Trotsky was so upset by what he saw as a usurpation of "his" newspaper's name that he wrote a letter, in April 1913, to Nikolay Chkheidz, a Menshevik leader, bitterly denouncing Lenin and the Bolsheviks. Later, when Trotsky began losing power in the early 1920s, the contents of the letter were made public by his opponents within the Communist Party and they were used to paint him as Lenin's enemy.

While in Vienna, Trotsky contributed articles on literature, painting and poetry under a variety of pseudonyms in radical newspapers like *Kievskaya Mysl*. In September 1912 Trotsky was sent by *Kievskaya Mysl* as its war correspondent to the Balkans, where for the next year he covered the two Balkan Wars. His interest in the wars was that of a revolutionary observer.

With the outbreak of World War One, Trotsky left Vienna and made his way to neutral Switzerland. He left Vienna on August 3, 1914, to avoid arrest as a Russian émigré. While in Switzerland, Trotsky briefly worked within the Swiss Socialist Party and wrote *The War and the International*. In the book he denounced the pro-war position taken by the European social democratic parties, primarily the German Social Democratic Party.

Trotsky moved to France on November 19, 1914, as a war correspondent for the *Kievskaya Mysl*. In January he began editing *Nashe Slovo* (*Our World*), an internationalist socialist newspaper in Paris. He continued to denounce the war and joined with pacifists in urging workers not to participate in the conflict. He adopted the slogan "peace without indemnities or annexations, peace without conquerors or conquered." His actions would cause him to be arrested by the French authorities and in September, 1916, he was deported to Spain.

The Spanish authorities would not permit him to stay and he was deported to the United States on December 25, 1916. He arrived in New York City on January 13, 1917. In New York, he wrote articles for the local Russian language socialist newspaper *Novy Mir* and for the Yiddish language daily *Der Forvents* (*The Forward*) in translation. He also made speeches to Russian émigrés.

World War One came to Russia in August 1914 when Germany declared war on Russia. Initially, the declaration of war produced unity and patriotic resolve within Russia. Virtually the entire Duma (the Russian Parliament) pledged to support Russia's war efforts and voted for war appropriations. The people believed that the war was being fought to defend Russia and, in the cities, Russian patriotism became anti-German. The capital city was renamed Petrograd because its former name, St. Petersburg, sounded too German.

The Russian military high command dispatched two armies into Germany's eastern Prussia, but the push forward was only temporary. Germany's military responded quickly and with their allies, the Austrians, drove the Russians out of Germany, through Poland and back into Russia. Hundreds of thousands of Russian soldiers lost their lives, and Russian morale was seriously damaged. In the fall of 1915, Tsar Nicholas II left Russia's capital city to take personal command of the Russian armies.

In his absence from the capital city, the tsar placed effective control of the Russian government in the hands of his wife, Alexandra. By this time the tsarina had fallen under the influence of Grigori Rasputin, a Siberian monk. To Alexandra, Rasputin was a holy man for he alone seemed able to stop the bleeding of her hemophiliac son, Alexis. Rasputin's influence over the tsarina made him an important power behind the throne, and he did not hesitate to interfere in government affairs. Ministers were appointed and dismissed on a word from Rasputin. By 1916, Rasputin's behavior had become so intolerable that three members of the high aristocracy, fearful for the survival of the monarchy, murdered the monk.

The death of Rasputin would not make a difference because by this time public confidence in the tsar's government had disappeared. Two years of Russian military defeats, millions of military casualties, shortages of food and fuel in the cities and government inefficiency and corruption had turned the people against the crown.

In March 1917, a series of strikes and demonstrations would bring to an end tsarist rule. In the month previous, the government had introduced bread rationing in Petrograd after the price of bread soared. Many of the women who stood in lines waiting for bread were also factory workers who labored twelve-hour days. On March 8, a day celebrated since 1910 as International Women's Day, thousands of Petrograd women marched through the capital city demanding "peace and bread" and chanting "down with autocracy." Soon the women were joined by other workers, and together they called for a general strike which succeeded in shutting down, on March 10, all the factories in the city. The tsarina informed her husband about these developments in a letter, and the tsar responded by demanding the adjournment of the Duma and ordering the police and the troops stationed in Petrograd to stop the striking crowds by shooting them if necessary. At first the soldiers obeyed, but soon a significant number of them joined the demonstrating crowds.

On March 12, some members of the Duma formed a provisional committee to keep order. Hostility toward the crown and demonstrations against the government had already spread to other cities. Alone and helpless, Tsar Nicholas II followed the advice of his generals and abdicated on March 15 in favor of his younger brother, Michael. He, in turn, abdicated in favor of the Duma's provisional committee. By this time the members of the committee considered themselves a provisional government. The three hundred year reign of the Romanov dynasty had come to an end, and Russia ceased to be a monarchy.

At first the Provisional Government enjoyed considerable support both at home and abroad. It disbanded the tsarist police, granted amnesty to political prisoners and allowed exiles to return home. It repealed all limitations on freedom of speech, press and association. It abolished laws that discriminated against ethnic or religious groups. It announced plans for social reforms and promised to summon a democratically elected constituent assembly which was to establish a permanent government by giving Russia a constitution. Russia's allies recognized, almost immediately, the Provisional Government as the legitimate governing body of Russia and began to supply it generously with war credits.

The two most important issues facing the Provisional Government were agrarian discontent and the continuation of the war. Russia's peasants wanted land, and they wanted it immediately. The Provisional Government, however, believed in acting with deliberation and according to the law. It refused to sanction peasant seizure of land despite the increasing disorder in the countryside. Instead, it appointed a commission to collect data on which future agrarian legislation was to be based. It was a decision that was inadequate to the emergency. As for the war, the members of the Provisional Government continued to honor the tsar's commitments to Russia's allies by participating in the fight against Germany and its allies. Most of the members hoped that Russia would win the war and gain the territories which had been promised to Russia.

When the Provisional Government was formed in March 1917, Lenin believed the opportunity had come for the Bolsheviks to seize power in Russia. In April 1917, Germany's Military High Command, calculating that Lenin's return to Russia would disrupt and undermine Russia's war effort, arranged to transport Lenin in a sealed train through Germany to the Baltic Sea coastline. From there he could be brought by ferry to Finland. Lenin, his wife and several trusted colleagues eventually arrived in Russia by way of Finland. Shortly after their arrival, they were joined by other Marxists who the tsarist government had formerly imprisoned or who had been forced to flee abroad.

In a series of proposals known as his "April Theses," issued on April 20, 1917, Lenin presented a blueprint for revolutionary action. In the "April Theses," Lenin maintained that the soviets of soldiers, workers and peasants were ready made instruments of power. The Bolsheviks must work to gain control of these groups and then use them to overthrow the Provisional Government. At the same time, Bolshevik propaganda must be used to gain mass support through promises: an end to the war, a redistribution of all land to the peasants, the transfer of factories and industries from capitalists to committees of workers, and the relegation of political power from the Provisional Government to the soviets. Three simple slogans summed up the Bolshevik program: "Peace, Land, Bread," "Workers Control of Production" and "All Power to the Soviets."

Trotsky made his way back to Russia on May 4, 1917. He decided to return after he learned that Tsar Nicholas II had stepped down from power. He left New York on March 27, 1917, but British naval officials in Halifax,

Nova Scotia intercepted his ship. He spent a month detained at Amherst, Nova Scotia. He was released upon the request of Pavel Miliukov, the Russian foreign minister representing the Provisional Government. The British government freed Trotsky on April 29 and less than a week later Trotsky was back in Russia.

Upon his return to Russia, Trotsky was neither a Menshevik nor a Bolshevik. He temporarily joined the Mezhraiontsky, a regional social democratic organization in Petrograd, and became one of its leaders. Trotsky disapproved of the support that many leading Mensheviks were now giving the Provisional Government and the Russian war effort. Instead, he decided to give his support to Lenin. He told Lenin that nothing separated him from Lenin's "April Theses." The two agreed, however, that Trotsky would not join the Bolshevik Party at once, but would wait until he (Trotsky) could bring as many of the Mezhraiontsky group into the Bolshevik ranks.

Between April and June 1917, the Bolshevik Party was engaged in recruiting new members and building support. It particularly wanted to extend its influence in the Petrograd Soviet, where the majority was still held by Menshevik and Socialist Revolutionary deputies. Lenin's preferred tactic was to wait patiently as the Bolshevik Party grew while at the same time attacking the government with propaganda and rhetoric and promoting the soviets as the alternative government. However, events in Petrograd in mid-1917 fueled the demand for popular revolution faster than Lenin preferred.

The Provisional Government's support for the war radicalized thousands of Russian soldiers. In mid-June 1917, Alexander Kerensky, the government's minister of war, approved a massive assault on the Austro-Hungarian defenses at Galicia. Kerensky hoped to improve morale, both in the ranks of the army and in Russia generally. The first two days of the "Kerensky Offensive", as it became known, were quite successful and the Russian infantrymen advanced through the Austro-Hungarian defenses. But the offensive soon encountered strong military resistance from German units and the Russians were stopped and pushed back. By mid-September the Germans had captured Riga and were advancing toward Petrograd.

News of the failed military offensive was met with anger and hostility in the cities. The Provisional Government's coalition ministry collapsed and the prime minister, Prince Georgi Lvov resigned. On the evening of July 3, street demonstrations and riots broke out in Petrograd involving thousands of factory workers. On the following day, the demonstrators and rioters were joined by mutinous soldiers from the Petrograd garrison, as well as sailors from the nearby island fortress of Kronstadt. A revolution was building, but who would lead it?

One large crowd of people assembled outside the Tauride Palace, the meeting place of the Petrograd Soviet. The crowd expected a declaration that the Soviet had assumed power. All they got, however, was the moderate

Socialist Revolutionary leader, Victor Chernov. He gave a series of excuses as to why the Provisional Government should re-form and continue. Chernov's equivocation angered the crowd, including one heckler, who famously shouted "Why don't you take power, you son of a bitch, when they're handing it to you on a plate?"[6]

Meanwhile, others were looking elsewhere for revolutionary leadership. A large group, comprised of factory workers and Kronstadt sailors, marched on the Kseshinskaya Palace, the temporary headquarters of the Bolshevik leadership. Outside the palace, they cheered and chanted for Lenin, expecting the Bolshevik leader to deliver a rousing speech calling for the overthrow of the Provisional Government. Lenin eventually appeared before them but his comments were brief, restrained and anticlimatic. The Bolshevik leader offered the crowd neither inspiration, instruction nor his full support. After Lenin finished speaking and withdrew, the deflated mob broke up and scattered across the city. Many of them resorted to heavy drinking, looting and vandalism. When government forces arrived from the military front a day later, they were able to crush the uprising without much opposition. Around 700 people were killed, most of them Bolsheviks or Bolshevik sympathizers.

The Provisional Government held Lenin and the Bolsheviks responsible for the July uprising. Kerensky, who in late July was appointed prime minister, took immediate action. He ordered the arrest of Lenin and authorized the publication of material claiming that the Bolshevik leader was receiving financial support from the Germans. Being painted as a traitor, Lenin's popularity began to erode and he was forced to flee from Russia, disguised as a fisherman, and take refuge in Finland. Hundreds of Bolsheviks were rounded up, imprisoned or forced into exile. Among those who were arrested was Trotsky. He was arrested on July 24, 1917; he had officially joined the Bolshevik Party in July.

Trotsky would be released from prison during an attempted military coup by General Lavr Kornilov. Kerensky, as prime minister, had named General Kornilov as the new commander-in-chief of the Russian Army. Kerensky asked General Kornilov to send troops to Petrograd to impose martial law and defend the Provisional Government against a future uprising. But when Kerensky was told that General Kornilov demanded the resignation of the cabinet of the Provisional Government and the surrender of all military and civil authority to the Russian Army, the prime minister reacted by dismissing General Kornilov from office and charging him with treason. Kornilov refused to resign and sent troops under the leadership of General Aleksandr Krymov to take control of Petrograd.

Kerensky, aware of the danger that he and his cabinet faced, approached the Petrograd Soviet with a deal. In return for their help in fighting off General Krymov's advancing forces, Kerensky agreed to release from prison the Bolsheviks who had been arrested earlier in July and to arm the Soviet forces with weapons from the government's armories. The Petrograd Soviet agreed to the arrangement and Trotsky was among those who were released from prison.

Upon their release from prison, the Bolsheviks used their influence over the railway and communication workers to disrupt Kornilov's military coup. They severed the supply lines and diverted the trains to prevent General Krymov's troops from reaching Petrograd. The military coup melted away before it ever reached Petrograd and Kornilov was arrested. However, the Petrograd Soviet troops, many of them Bolshevik Red Guards, refused to hand back the guns and ammunition that they were given by the government and the episode left Lenin's supporters well armed.

The Kornilov affair allowed the Bolshevik movement to recover from its July setback. Though Lenin was still in Finland, Trotsky and other Bolshevik leaders went about rebuilding the Party's organizational structure. They stepped up their anti-war campaign and their anti-government propaganda and succeeded in attracting greater levels of support. At the beginning of 1917, the Bolsheviks had just 24,000 card-carrying members; by the end of September they had more than 400,000 members. The growth in support was reflected in the soviets where the Bolsheviks gained voting majorities in both Petrograd and Moscow. The Red Guards, the Bolshevik militia, now had around 100,000 men, mostly factory workers and current or former soldiers. The path was cleared for yet another Russian revolution.

The push for an immediate seizure of power came from Lenin. The Bolshevik leader penned from Finland several letters to his colleagues in Russia urging them to overthrow the Provisional Government as soon as possible. To delay would be fatal, Lenin argued, offering the following scenarios: Kerensky may submit to another Kornilov and impose martial law; the support for the Bolsheviks might peak and then tumble; Petrograd might fall to the Germans. Within the Bolshevik hierarchy there was some opposition to Lenin's urgent call for immediate revolution. Lev Kamenev and Grigori Zinoviev both dismissed Lenin's arguments. Lenin's call for revolution was premature, they argued, and would create a Bolshevik government that was fragile and unlikely to survive.

Trotsky supported Lenin's push for an immediate seizure of power. He was now the chairman of the Petrograd Soviet, a position that was handed to him after the Bolsheviks became the majority in the Soviet. In early October, Trotsky called for the formation of the Military Revolutionary Committee (Milrevcom or MRC) to plot the overthrow of the government. The members of the Petrograd Soviet passed Trotsky's resolution; the Military Revolutionary Committee was formed and Trotsky was its chairman and de facto leader. Through the middle of October, Trotsky worked to arm the Bolshevik Red Guard units and bring them under the control of the Military Revolutionary

Committee. This was done in preparation for the upcoming Bolshevik Revolution.

The second attempt by the Bolsheviks to remove the Provisional Government from power came relatively easy. Beginning on November 4 (Gregorian calendar) or October 22 (Julian calendar), large demonstrations and mass meetings were addressed by Trotsky. His actions were supported by Lenin who, by this time, had returned to Petrograd, after spending weeks in hiding in Finland. Kerensky was also on the move. He left Petrograd in a car and made his way to Russia's military frontline in a desperate attempt to recruit troops to return with him to Petrograd to defend the government. He was unsuccessful and did not return to Petrograd. On November 7 (Gregorian calendar), Bolshevik Red Guard units and troops loyal to the Petrograd Soviet, organized by the Military Revolutionary Committee, captured in Petrograd critical installations and infrastructure: government buildings, armories, telegram stations, bridges and thorough fares. The next day they surrounded and stormed the Winter Palace, the headquarters of the Provisional Government, and arrested the government's cabinet members. The Provisional Government fell almost without resistance. In less than twenty-four hours, the Bolsheviks had carried out successfully their revolution. Although the Bolshevik Revolution took place in November (Gregorian calendar), in Russia it was commonly called the October Revolution. (See Glossary- October Revolution)

On the afternoon of November 8 (Gregorian Calendar) or October 26 (Julian Calendar), Lenin announced to the National Congress of Soviets in Petrograd that he was transferring the political sovereignty of the Provisional Government to that body. The National Congress of Soviets represented the local soviets from all over the country. Lenin then maneuvered the National Congress of Soviets to accept the Council of People's Commissars as the executive body of the new government. The Bolsheviks occupied the top positions in the Council of People's Commissars. Lenin held the post of chairman, and Trotsky became the People's Commissar for Foreign Affairs. Lenin pledged to build a socialist state.

Confident that the majority of Russia's people favored their policies, the Bolsheviks allowed elections by universal male suffrage to be held for a constituent assembly. However, they were shocked when they learned that they polled only about a quarter of the votes while their main adversaries, the Socialist Revolutionaries, polled more than sixty percent of the votes. The delegates elected to the constituent assembly met only once, on January 18, 1918 (Gregorian calendar). The following day Lenin dissolved it by decree and sent guards bearing rifles to prevent it from ever meeting again. The anti-Bolshevik majority in the constituent assembly was furious at Lenin's act of pure force against the popular will, but there was no public outburst and the delegates did disband.

One of Lenin's primary goals was to end Russia's war against Germany. Trotsky, as People's Commissar for Foreign Affairs, was head of the Soviet delegation during the peace negotiations with the Germans which began in December 1917. The Germans, aware of Russia's helplessness, demanded among other things, Finland, the Ukraine, Poland and the Baltic states. If Germany's demands were met, Russia would lose more than a million square kilometers of territory, including a third of its arable land and one third of its population. It would also lose three-quarters of its deposits of iron and coal and about one quarter of its heavy industries. Trotsky refused to sign on Germany's harsh terms and on February 10, 1918, he withdrew from the talks and returned to Russia.

After a brief hiatus, the Germans notified the Soviet government that they would no-longer observe the existing truce after February 17. The Germans meant it and resumed their military operations on February 18. Lenin balked at Germany's demands, but with the German military advancing into Russia and the failure of the recently formed Red Army to resist the German offensive, he believed that he had no other option but to agree to Germany's demands. The treaty that took Russia out of the war was signed at Brest-Litovsk on March 3, 1918. Two days later, Lenin moved his government to Moscow, the center of Russia.

After the signing of the Treaty of Brest-Litovsk, Russia plunged into a civil war. Throughout Russia there emerged groups that were hostile to the Bolsheviks who now called themselves the Russian Communist Party. Lenin changed the name of his party in 1918 because the word communist implied a concern for the human community. The counterrevolutionaries, collectively called "Whites," were led by former tsarist military officers and included members of the outlawed nobility, former landowners, supporters of the tsar and socialists from rival parties, including the Mensheviks and Socialist Revolutionaries.

By late June 1918, Russia's allies of World War One intervened in the Russian Civil War on behalf of the opponents of the Communists. The Japanese occupied Russia's far eastern provinces, while the French, British and Americans sent supplies as well as troops to aid the "White" forces. The Allies were eager to see the "Whites" win the civil war, not only to prevent the spread of Communism but also because they hoped that under different political leadership, Russia would reenter the war against Germany.

To meet the new danger, Trotsky was placed in full control of the Red Army. On March 13, 1918, Trotsky's resignation as Commissar for Foreign Affairs was officially accepted and he was appointed People's Commissar of Army and Navy Affairs. With the assistance of his faithful deputy, Ephraim Sklyansky, Trotsky spent the rest of the civil war transforming the Red Army from a ragtag network of small and independent detachments into a large and disciplined military machine. Trotsky reinstated the draft and increased the size of the Red Army from less than 300,000 in May 1918 to one million in October 1918. He recruited and gave commands to former tsarist army officers and brought into the Red Army political commissars. The latter were responsible for ensuring that the military officers to whom they were assigned were loyal to the Soviet government; they co-signed the orders of the military commanders. Trotsky insisted on rigid discipline and introduced severe penalties for insubordination. He organized the formation of the infamous "blocking units," special squads stationed behind the front-line troops, whose role it was to summarily gun down all soldiers suspected of desertion and unauthorized retreat. Trotsky threatened to execute the commanders and commissars whose units either deserted or retreated without permission.

Trotsky believed that State-sponsored propagation of revolutionary ideals could improve an army's performance. Thus, using a personal armored train, he would visit the most critical sections of the military fronts. While there, he not only planned and supervised military operations but used his oratorical talents to inspire the Red Army soldiers. Trotsky made at least 36 trips to hot spots in 1918–1920. His train carried a radio transmitter, a printing press for on the site production of propaganda, a generous supply of tobacco to be distributed to the soldiers and a brass band, all to boost morale. Trotsky's train became one of the symbols of the Red Army.

During the Russian Civil War, Trotsky's Red Army was forced to fight on several fronts. The first serious threat to the Communist regime came from Siberia where a "White" army under Admiral Alexander Kolchak pushed westward and advanced almost to the Volga River before being stopped. The regime's worst crisis during the civil war came in October of 1919. General Anton Denikin's "White" Russian forces were approaching Tula and Moscow from the south and General Nikolay Yudenich's troops were approaching Petrograd from the west. Lenin believed that it was more important to defend Moscow, Lenin's new capital, and that Petrograd would have to be abandoned. Trotsky argued that Petrograd needed to be defended and his position prevailed against Lenin in the Central Committee of the Russian Communist Party. Trotsky immediately went to Petrograd in his train and organized its defense. By October 22, the Red Army was on the offensive and in early November Yudenich's troops were driven back to Estonia, where they were disarmed and interned. Trotsky was awarded the Order of the Red Banner for his actions in Petrograd. (see Glossary—Order of the Red Banner)

The Communists were equally successful in crushing political opposition in the territories under their control. Following a failed assassination attempt on Lenin by a Socialist Revolutionary named Dora Kaplan in 1918, the Communists initiated a Red Terror campaign. It was conducted by Felix Dzerzhinsky the chief of a newly organized secret police force, the All-Russian Extraordinary Commission for the Struggle against Counterrevolution and Sabotage, known by its acronym of CHEKA. The agents of CHEKA arrested, tried and executed anyone known to be or suspected of being hostile to the Communists. The place of enemies, in Lenin's words, was "against the wall." CHEKA killed thousands of people. In order to prevent organized political opposition, Lenin's government outlawed all political parties except the Russian Communist Party, thereby converting Russia into a one-party dictatorship.

In December 1922 the Union of Soviet Socialist Republics was formally established. Commonly called the Soviet Union, it was a federal union consisting of territories, regions, nominally autonomous states and republics. Of the four republics, the Russian Soviet Federated Socialist Republic (Russia) was the largest and the most influential. The other three were the Transcaucasian Soviet Federated Socialist Republic (Armenia, Azerbaijan and Georgia), the Ukrainian Soviet Socialist Republic (Ukraine) and the Belorussian Soviet Socialist Republic (Belorussia). As time went on, the boundaries of the republics would shift and the number of republics would increase.

The Communists formalized their authoritarian rule in a constitution drafted in 1924. The constitution granted the franchise to all productive workers over the age of eighteen but not to the bourgeoisie or to those closely identified with tsarism and the Russian Orthodox Church. The Party leadership demonstrated their distrust of the Russian peasants by making each urban vote of the electorate equivalent to five rural votes. Ostensibly, political power rested with the elected local soviets that were organized according to occupation. These soviets elected delegates to the Congress of Soviets of their canton, the smallest administrative unit, and each of these congresses in turn sent delegates to a congress at the next administrative level. The supreme body of government authority was the All-Union Congress of Soviets. It was to meet at least once in two years. Because the All-Union Congress of Soviets was not a permanent body, the members (delegates) elected an executive committee to act in their behalf between sessions. The executive committee was called the Central Executive Committee.

The Central Executive Committee was to meet three times a year. During the interval between sessions of the Central Executive Committee, the Presidium of the Committee supervised the government administration. Finally, the Central Executive Committee elected the Council of People's Commissars, which served as the executive arm of the government. The members of the Council of People's Commissars were elected for a two-year term. The Council was commonly called Sovnarkom which is an abbreviation for Soviet narodnykh kommissarov (Council of People's Commissars).

The constitution did not mention the Russian Communist Party, but the Party was the real center of political power. The central Party institutions included the Party Congress, the Central Committee, the Politburo (political bureau), the Secretariat and the Party commissions. The Party Congress was expected to convene every year for about a week. It was attended by delegates who had been elected by republic Party congresses or by conferences of territories, provinces and autonomous republics. While in session, the Party Congress voted on several kinds of issues and all decisions were unanimous.

Most important, the Party Congress formally elected the members of the Central Committee, which it charged to govern the Party until the next Party Congress. The Party leadership drew up a list of candidates and presented it to the Party Congress for ratification. Both personal merit and institutional affiliation determined the selection of candidates; the majority were selected because of the positions they held. But because the Central Committee was too large and cumbersome to perform its duties, it delegated its authority to the Politburo.

The Politburo was established two weeks before the Bolshevik Revolution in 1917. It was formed as a means to centralize decision making. Since the revolution, it consisted of the highest Party and government officials in the Soviet Union. The Politburo was composed of full (voting) members and of candidate (non-voting) members. In 1922 the Politburo was made up of seven full (voting) members: Vladimir Lenin, Leon Trotsky, Joseph Stalin, Grigory Zinoviev, Lev Kamenev, Alexie Rykov and Mikhail Tomsky. The three candidate (non-voting) members were Nikolai Bukharin, Mikhail Kalinin and Vyacheslav Molotov. The Politburo was the highest decision making body in the Soviet Union. It made all the major policy decisions for both the Party and the government.

Lenin's health began to deteriorate after Dora Kaplan shot him in 1918. Severe headaches limited his sleep and he began to suffer from fatigue. Lenin decided he needed someone to control the Communist Party. At the Party Conference in April 1922, Lenin suggested that a new post of General Secretary should be created. The man who was chosen for this post was Joseph Stalin.

Born Joseph Djugashvili in 1879 in the Georgian region of Transcaucasia, Stalin was the son of a poor shoemaker. Admitted to a seminary to be trained for the priesthood, young Stalin was later expelled for holding radical opinions. He joined the Bolsheviks in 1903 and came to Lenin's attention after staging a daring bank robbery to obtain funds for the Bolshevik cause. In 1912, Lenin made Stalin a member of the Bolshevik's Central Committee and in that same year told him to write a work on Marxism and nationalism, which Stalin completed to Lenin's satisfaction. In 1917, Stalin arrived in Petrograd about three weeks before Lenin and worked as editor of the Bolshevik paper, *Pravda*. In 1922, he became General Secretary of the Communist Party's Central Committee. As General Secretary, Stalin prepared the agenda for Politburo meetings; he supplied the documentation for points under debate and passed the decisions made by the Politburo down to the lower levels.

Soon after Stalin's appointment as General Secretary, Lenin went into a hospital to have a bullet removed from his body; it had been there since Kaplan's assassination attempt. It was hoped that this operation would restore his health. This would not be the case. Soon afterwards, a blood vessel broke in Lenin's brain. It left Lenin paralyzed down his right side and for some time he was unable to speak. As Lenin's assistant, Stalin had suddenly become very important.

While Lenin was immobilized, Stalin made full use of his powers as General Secretary. At the Party Congress, he had been granted permission to expel unsatisfactory Party members. As General Secretary, Stalin also had the authority to appoint people to and remove people from important positions in the government. The new holders of government posts were fully aware that they owed their positions to Stalin. They also knew that if their behavior did not please Stalin, they would be replaced.

Surrounded by his supporters, Stalin's confidence began to grow. In October 1922, he disagreed with Lenin over the issue of foreign trade. When the matter was discussed at the Party's Central Committee, Stalin's policy rather than Lenin's was accepted. Fearing that Stalin was taking over the leadership of the Party, Lenin wrote Trotsky asking for his support. Trotsky agreed and at the next meeting of the Party's Central Committee the decision on foreign trade was reversed. Lenin, who was too ill to attend, wrote to Trotsky congratulating him on his success and suggesting that in the future they should work together against Stalin.

Stalin learned about the contents of Lenin's letter to Trotsky from his (Stalin's) wife, Nadezhda Alliluyeva, who worked in Lenin's private office. Stalin was furious as he realized that if Lenin and Trotsky worked together against him, his political career would come to an end. In a fit of temper, Stalin made an abusive telephone call to Lenin's wife, Nadezhda Krupskaya, accusing her of endangering Lenin's life by allowing him to write letters when he was so ill.

After Nadezhda told her husband of the phone call, Lenin made the decision that Stalin was not the man to replace him as the leader of the Party. Lenin knew that he was close to death so he dictated to his secretary a letter that he wanted to serve as his last will and testament. He wrote: "Having become General Secretary, Comrade Stalin has concentrated immeasurable power in his hands and I am not sure that he will always know how to use that power with sufficient caution. . . . On the other hand, Comrade Trotsky . . . has distinguished himself not only by his outstanding abilities. . . . He is certainly the ablest man on the present Committee, but is possessed of excessive self-confidence and has a disposition to be too much attracted by the purely administrative aspect of affairs. . . . These characteristics of the two most eminent leaders of the present Central Committee may, unintentionally, lead to a split if the Party does not take measures to prevent it. . . ."[7]

On the fourth of January, 1923, Lenin added a postscript to his earlier testament: "Stalin is too rude, and this fault . . . becomes intolerable in the office of General Secretary. . . . I invite the comrades to consider ways of removing Stalin from this post and appointing somebody who is better in all respects than Stalin, namely one more tolerant, more loyal, more polite, more considerate towards his comrades, less capricious, etc."[8]

Three days after writing the above testament, Lenin suffered a third stroke. Lenin was no longer able to speak or write. Although he lived for another ten months, he ceased to exist as a political power within the Soviet Union. It was assumed that Trotsky would replace Lenin as the leader of the Communist Party.

To prevent Trotsky's rise to leadership, Stalin established a triumvirate composed of himself and two "old Bolsheviks," Grigory Zinoviev and Lev Kamenev. The latter two had joined the Russian Social Democratic Labor Party in 1901. Both joined Lenin's faction, the Bolsheviks, within the party in 1903 and both were with Lenin in Petrograd at the time of the Bolshevik Revolution in 1917. By 1921 Zinoviev had become the head of the Petrograd Party organization, the chairman of the Petrograd Soviet and a member of the Politburo of the Communist Party. He was also the chairman of the executive committee of the Communist International (Comintern). Kamenev became a member of the Politburo in 1919 and was chairman of the Moscow Soviet.

Isaac Deutscher, the author of *Stalin* published in 1949, pointed out: "What made for the solidarity of the three men was their determination to prevent Trotsky from succeeding to the leadership of the party [Party]. Separately, neither could measure up to Trotsky. Jointly, they represented a powerful combination of talent and influence. Zinoviev was the politician, the orator, the demagogue with popular appeal. Kamenev was the strategist of the group, its solid brain, trained in matters of doctrine, which were to play a paramount part in the contest for power. Stalin was the tactician of the triumvirate and its organizing force. Between them, the three men virtually controlled the whole party [Party], through it, the Government."[9]

Trotsky and his supporters, together known as the Left Opposition, criticized Stalin and his allies. They accused them of turning the Party into a dictatorship. They demanded a restoration of Party democracy. Trotsky expressed his concern on the fifth of December, 1923, in a published open letter in which he called for more debate in the Party concerning the way the country was being governed. He argued that Party members should exercise their right to criticize "without fear." He further argued that the first people who needed to be removed from the Party should be "those who at the first voice of criticism, of objection, of protest, are inclined to demand one's party ticket for the purpose of repression." Trotsky went on to suggest that anyone who "dares to terrorize the party" should be expelled from the Party.[10]

Zinoviev was furious with Trotsky for making the above comments and proposed that he should be arrested immediately. Stalin, aware of Trotsky's immense popularity, opposed the move as being too dangerous. He did, however, encourage Zinoviev and Kamenev to attack Trotsky.

Stalin waited until the end of December, 1923, before addressing the issue of Party democracy raised by Trotsky and the Left Opposition. Stalin did not believe that the Party was a debating society. Debate, he argued, would lead to the creation of factions and groupings within the Party. Without mentioning Trotsky, Stalin asked the question: "Did the opposition [Trotsky and his supporters] demand that Lenin's rules, which banned factions and groupings inside the party, should be abolished?"[11]

Lenin died on January 21, 1924, and following his death there emerged the cult of Lenin. Inspired by genuine reverence and by a political desire to move the masses around a potent symbol, the members of the Politburo had Lenin's body embalmed and placed in a sarcophagus inside a mausoleum for public viewing. The mausoleum, designed as a cube-like structure and made of red granite, was built on Red Square in front of the Kremlin Wall in Moscow. Outside of the mausoleum a large number of people daily would stand in line for hours to enter and view the mummified body of Lenin. The writings of Lenin became sacred and irrefutable. Images of the father of the Soviet Union appeared everywhere in stone and metal, on canvas and in print. Lenin corners, analogous to the icon corners of Russian Orthodoxy, became fixtures in nearly every Soviet institution, and Lenin's name graced thousands of libraries, schools and streets. On January 25, 1924, just five days after Lenin's death, Petrograd (St. Petersburg) was renamed Leningrad, meaning city of Lenin.

Trotsky's main hope of gaining power was for Lenin's last testament to be published. In May, 1924, Lenin's widow, Nadezhda Krupskaya, demanded that the Central Committee of the Party announce its contents to the rest of the Party. Zinoviev argued strongly against its publication. He finished his speech with the words: "You have all witnessed our harmonious cooperation in the last few months; and, like myself, you will be happy to say that Lenin's fears have proved baseless."[12] The new members of the Party's Central Committee, who had been sponsored by Stalin, guaranteed that the vote went against Lenin's testament being made public.

On November 19 of 1924, Stalin felt strong enough to denounce Trotsky directly and publicly in a speech that he made to the plenum (a full assembly) of the Communist group in the All Union Central Council of Trade Unions (A.U.C.C.T.U.). In the speech, Stalin defined what he labeled Trotskyism and he explained how it differed from Leninism. The three features of Trotskyism according to Stalin were:

First, "Trotskyism is the theory of 'permanent' [uninterrupted] revolution. But what is permanent revolution in its Trotskyist interpretation? It is revolution that fails to take the poor peasantry into account as a revolutionary force. Trotsky's 'permanent' revolution is, as Lenin said, 'skipping' the peasant movement 'playing the seizure of power.' Why is it dangerous? Because such a revolution, if an attempt had been made to bring it about, would inevitably have ended in failure, for it would have divorced from the Russian proletariat its ally, the poor peasantry."

Second, "Trotskyism is distrust of the Bolshevik Party principle, of the monolithic character of the Party, of its hostility towards opportunist elements. In the sphere of organization, Trotskyism is the theory that revolutionaries and opportunists can co-exit and form groups and coteries within a single party."

Third, "Trotskyism is distrust of the leaders of Bolshevism, an attempt to discredit, to defame them. I do not know of a single trend in the Party that could compare with Trotskyism in the matter of discrediting the leaders of Leninism or the central institutions of the Party."

Seven days later, on November 26, 1924, Stalin's speech titled "Trotskyism or Leninism?" was published in Pravda.[13]

Nine years later, in 1933, Stalin elaborated on the three features of Trotskyism in the second volume of his written work entitled *Leninism*. (See Document One)

In January 1925, the triumvirate was able to force Trotsky to resign as People's Commissar of Army and Navy Affairs and as Chairman of the Revolutionary Military Council. Some of Trotsky's supporters pleaded with him to organize a military coup d'etat but Trotsky rejected the idea. Deutscher, the author of *Stalin* (1949) maintained: "He left office without the slightest attempt at rallying in his defense the army he had created and led for seven years. He still regarded the party, no matter how or by whom it was led, as the legitimate spokesman of the working class."[14]

The year 1925 proved to be an unusual year for Trotsky. After losing his Red Army posts, he was effectively unemployed throughout the winter and spring. In May he was given three posts: chairman of the Concessions Committee, head of the electro-technical board and chairman of the scientific-technical board of industry. Trotsky wrote in *My Life* (1930) that he "was taking a rest from politics" and "naturally plunged into his new line of work." Later in the year, Trotsky resigned from his two technical positions and concentrated on his work in the Concessions Committee.

In the meantime, Kamenev and Zinoviev had broken with Stalin over issues such as building "socialism in one country." It was a thesis formulated by Nikolai Bukharin, the leading Party theoretician and editor of *Pravda*. Bukharin argued that socialism could be developed in a single country, even in one as underdeveloped as Russia. Bukharin stated that revolution need not be encouraged in the world's capitalist countries since Russia could and should achieve socialism alone. "Socialism in one country" was adopted by Stalin and it became a hallmark of Stalinism.

What Stalin told the Party was this: "Of course we are looking forward to international revolution. Of course we have been brought up in the school of Marxism; and we know that contemporary social and political struggles are, by their very nature, international. Of course we still believe the victory of the proletariat in the west to be near; and we are bound in honor to do what we can to speed it up. But . . . do not worry so much about all that international revolution. Even if it were to be delayed indefinitely, even if it were never to occur, we in this country [Soviet Russia] are capable of developing into a fully fledged, classless society. Let us then concentrate on our great constructive task. Those who tell you that this is utopia, that I am preaching national narrow-mindedness, are themselves either adventurers or pusillanimous Social Democrats. We . . . have already done more for socialism than the proletariat of all other countries taken together; and, left alone . . . we shall do the rest of the job."[15]

How can a country like Russia achieve socialism? Stalin pointed to Russia's great assets: her vast spaces and enormous riches in raw materials. A proletarian government could, in his view, through its control of industry and credit, develop those resources and carry the building of socialism to a successful conclusion, because in this endeavor it would be supported by a vast majority of the people, including the peasants. Stalin's answer to the question was clear and positive. "We," he asserted, "are able to stand on our own feet, to build and to complete the building of socialism."[16]

After Kamenev and Zinoviev broke away from Stalin, they formed what was called the New Opposition. However, they were defeated quickly by Stalin. The latter was supported by Bukharin and Alexie Rykov at the fourteenth Party Congress held in December 1925. Rykov was the deputy chairman of the Council of People's Commissars also known as Sovnarkom.

Following their defeat, Kamenev and Zinoviev, in an attempt to subvert Stalin's growing influence, joined Trotsky and his Left Opposition in what became known as the United Opposition. But by 1926 it was already too late to mount a strong challenge to Stalin's growing power. Through skillful maneuvering, Stalin had been able increasingly to secure control over the Party apparatus, eroding what little power base the oppositionists had.

At the end of the fifteenth Party Conference held in October 1926, Trotsky was removed from the Politburo. A year later, again in October, Trotsky and Zinoviev were removed from the Central Committee of the Party. On November 15, 1927, it was announced that Trotsky and Zinoviev were purged from the Party and in the following month the fifteenth Party Congress declared that Trotskyist views and the Left Opposition were incompatible with Party membership. Thereafter, all leading oppositionists, including Kamenev, were expelled from the Party.

After their expulsion by the fifteenth Party Congress, Kamenev, Zinoviev and their supporters surrendered to Stalin "admitting their mistakes" and renouncing their alliance with Trotsky and the Left Opposition. They were readmitted to the Communist Party in 1928. Trotsky and most of his followers, on the other hand, refused to bow to Stalin and were exiled to Siberia and Central Asia. Trotsky was exiled to Alma Ata in January 1928.

A year later, on January 20, 1929, Trotsky was informed that he was to be expelled from the Soviet Union. The decision was communicated to him by GPU agents as follows: "Considered: the case of Citizen Trotsky, Leon Davidovich, under Article 58/10 of the Criminal Code, on a charge of counterrevolutionary activity expressing itself in the organization of an illegal anti-Soviet party, whose activity has lately been directed toward provoking anti-Soviet actions and preparing for an armed struggle against the Soviet power. Resolved: Citizen Trotsky, Leon Davidovich, to be deported from the territory of the U.S.S.R."[17] Trotsky was accompanied by his wife Natalia Sedova and his son Lyova (Leon Sedov was his full adult name).

As Trotsky was still advocating world revolution, most countries refused to invite him in. His first station in exile was the Turkish island of Prinkipo, off the coast of Istanbul. There he stayed for four years. While living on the island, in 1929, Trotsky wrote three volumes of *My Life (1879–1929)* and during the next year the four long volumes of the *History of the Russian Revolution.* He also began a biography of Lenin but only completed Part I. The books were published in French, English, German and Russian as well as in several other languages. In February 1932, the Politburo announced that Trotsky and the members of his family who lived outside of the Soviet Union had been stripped of their Soviet citizenship.

In 1933 the Premier of France, Edouard Daladier, offered Trotsky asylum in France. He stayed first at Royan, then at Barbizon. He was not allowed to visit Paris. In 1935, it was implied to him that he was no longer welcome in France.

After considering alternatives, Trotsky and his wife moved to Norway, having received permission from the Minister of Justice, Mr. Trygve Lie, to enter the country. In Norway, Trotsky and his wife were guests of Konrad Knudsen and his wife near Oslo and Trotsky authored *The Revolution Betrayed* (1936). The book was a critique of the Soviet Union under Stalinism. Trotsky argued that the Soviet Union had degenerated into a state controlled by an undemocratic bureaucracy. He believed that it would either be overthrown by way of a political revolution which would establish a workers' democracy or it would degenerate to the point where the bureaucracy converted itself into a capitalist class.

In 1936 the Soviet Union informed the government of Norway that Trotsky's continued presence in Norway "was likely to impair friendly relations between the two countries."[18] Thereafter, Trygve Lie demanded from Trotsky a signed written declaration that he agree to refrain from writing about current political events that were taking place in the Soviet Union. (Trotsky was editing a Russian periodical titled *Opposition Bulletin* published in Paris by his son Leon Sedov.) Trotsky told Trygve Lie that he would not keep silent and he would continue to denounce Stalin's crimes. (By this time Stalin had initiated the Great Terror during which millions of Soviet citizens were arrested by the Soviet secret police, the NKVD.) Trotsky and his wife were placed under house arrest. But where were they to go?

The writer Antonio Hidalgo and the painter Diego Rivera approached the Mexican President, General Lazaro Cardenas, on Trotsky's behalf. President Cardenas decided to give Trotsky and his wife asylum and in December 1936 the couple left Norway by boat. On their arrival in Mexico, they lived as guests for a while in the house of Rivera. In time, they rented a large house in Coyoacan. The place was "isolated; on one side there was a wide stream . . . and on the other a dusty road with some Mexican adobe hovels." They built a wall around the grounds and a "visitor had to pass through a solid iron gate which a comrade would only open if he had received explicitly instructions and after he had examined the visitor through a spy-hole."[19]

Trotsky remained busy. He would shut himself up in his study and emerge only for meals. He wrote letters, articles and books and he outlined drafts of future work. Most of the time, he would dictate to a Russian secretary. He authored *Stalin's Crimes*, a work of 376 pages, published in Paris.[20] He signed a contract with Harpers Publishers for a biography of Stalin and was deeply preoccupied with this new manuscript when he was assassinated.

Trotsky was murdered by a Soviet agent whose name was Jacson Mornard, more commonly known as Ramon Mercader. He successfully attacked Trotsky in his study driving a pick of an ice axe into Trotsky's skull on August 20, 1940. Mornard had arrived in Mexico in January 1940 and was introduced to Trotsky some time in May. From then on, Trotsky and his wife opened freely to Mornard the gate at the house. On August 20 Mornard arrived at Coyoacan bringing with him a typed article he had written and the ice axe concealed in his rain coat. Trotsky invited Mornard into his study and minutes later Trotsky's wife heard a "terrible piercing cry. Trotsky appeared, leaning against the door-frame. His face was covered with blood . . . and his arms hung limply by his side." Trotsky told his wife as she "mopped the blood from his face and put ice on the wound in his head" that Mornard should not be killed. (Mornard had been wrestled down by three of Trotsky's assistants who were also his bodyguards.) "He must . . . talk," Trotsky insisted.[21] Thereafter, Trotsky was taken to a local hospital where he died the next day, August 21, 1940.

NOTES

1. Theodor Herzl, The Jewish State (New York: American Zionist Emergency Council, 1946), 86–87.
2. Herzl, The Jewish State, 92–93.
3. Herzl, The Jewish State, 96.
4. Leon Trotsky, My Life, An Attempt at an Autobiography (New York: Pathfinder Press, Inc. 1970), 152–53.
5. Victor Serge and Natalia Sedova Trotsky, The Life and Death of Leon Trotsky, trans. Arnold J. Pomerans (Chicago, Illinois: Haymarket Books, 2015), 68–69.
6. Serge and Trotsky, The Life and Death of Leon Trotsky, 40.
7. Serge and Trotsky, The Life and Death of Leon Trotsky, 113.
8. Serge and Trotsky, The Life and Death of Leon Trotsky, 114.
9. Isaac Deutscher, Stalin: A Political Biography (Oxford, England: Oxford University Press, 1949), 255.
10. Deutscher, Stalin: A Political Biography, 264.
11. Deutscher, Stalin: A Political Biography, 265.
12. Deutscher, Stalin: A Political Biography, 272.
13. Pravda, November 26, 1924.
14. Deutscher, Stalin: A Political Biography, 297.
15. Deutscher, Stalin: A Political Biography, 290.
16. Deutscher, Stalin: A Political Biography, 284–285.
17. Serge and Trotsky, The Life and Death of Leon Trotsky, 161.
18. Serge and Trotsky, The Life and Death of Leon Trotsky, 251.
19. Serge and Trotsky, The Life and Death of Leon Trotsky, 251.
20. Serge and Trotsky, The Life and Death of Leon Trotsky, 218.
21. Serge and Trotsky, The Life and Death of Leon Trotsky, 267.

Documents

DOCUMENT 1

"What is the essence of Trotskyism?" Stalin asked, in 1933, and he found it consisted in the following:

> "The essence of Trotskyism consists, first of all, in the denial of the possibility of building Socialism in the U.S.S.R., with the forces of the working class and the peasantry of our country. What does this mean? It means that if, in the near future, help does not come in the form of a victorious world revolution, we shall have to capitulate to the bourgeoisie and clear the road for a bourgeois-democratic republic. Consequently, we have here the bourgeois repudiation of the possibility of building Socialism in our country masked by 'revolutionary' phrase mongering about the victory of the world revolution. . . .
>
> "The essence of Trotskyism consists, secondly, in denying the possibility of drawing the basic masses of the peasantry into Socialist construction in the countryside. What does this mean? It means that the working class is not strong enough to lead the peasantry after it in the task of shunting the individual peasant farms on to collective rails and that, if in the near future the victory of the world revolution does not come to the aid of the working class, the peasantry will restore the old bourgeois system. Consequently, we have here the bourgeois denial of the strength and opportunities of the proletarian dictatorship for leading the peasantry to Socialism, covered with the mask of 'revolutionary' phrases about the victory of the world revolution. . . .
>
> "The essence of Trotskyism consists, lastly, in the denial of the necessity of iron discipline in the Party, in the recognition of the freedom of factional groupings in the Party, in the recognition of the necessity of constituting a Trotskyist party. For Trotskyism, the Communist Party of the Soviet Union must be not a united and single militant Party, but a collection of groups and factions, each with its own central organization, press and so forth. And what

does this mean? It means that following the freedom of political groupings in the Party must come the freedom of political parties in the country, *i.e.*, bourgeois democracy. Consequently, we have here the recognition of the freedom of factional groupings in the Party, leading directly to the toleration of political parties in the country of the dictatorship of the proletariat, and all covered up with phrases about 'internal Party democracy' and 'improving the regime' within the Party." (Joseph Stalin, *Leninism*, Vol. II, English Edition, New York: International Publishers, 1933. pp. 391–393.)

DOCUMENT 2

GREAT SOVIET ENCLYCLOPEDIA, 1947
TROFONEVROZY—TROCKIZM [Column 42]

TROTSKYISM. "Contemporary Trotskyism is not a political tendency in the working class, but [rather] an unprincipled, ideal-less band of wreckers, saboteurs, agents, spies, murderers, a band of accursed enemies of the working class, acting for hire of intelligence organs of foreign governments." (Stalin, "On deficiencies of Party work in Measures for the liquidation of Trotskyites and other double-dealers," 1937, P.14).

In the past, T. was an anti-Leninist, opportunist tendency and a most dangerous agency of the imperialist bourgeoisie in the workers' movement, a vilest variety of Menshevism. T. was the most important group implanting *centrism* (cf).

In the course of struggling against the ACP (b) [All-union Communist Party (Bolsheviks)], Trotskyism stopped being a political tendency in the working class and turned into the leading unit of the counterrevolutionary bourgeoisie, leading the struggle against Soviet power and the construction of socialism in the USSR, against Communism.

Trotsky always conducted a treasonable battle against Leninism, against the Party of Lenin and Stalin. At the second Congress of the RSDRP (1903) Trotsky together with the Mensheviks struggled against the Bolsheviks. On the question of the first paragraph of the charter of the party Trotsky defended the Menshevik formulation of [Julius] Martov and heatedly came out against the formulation of Lenin, struggling for the founding of a monolithic, militant, clearly organized party. Trotsky, in essence, rejected the dictatorship of the proletariat. After the Second Congress of the party, Trotsky, together with the Mensheviks, in every possible way subverted Bolshevik party-solidarity, frustrated the decisions of the Congress, trying to seize the leading centers of the party and disorganize party work.

In the period of the Russo-Japanese War and the first Russian Revolution (1904–7) Trotsky slid into the position of "defensism": he was against the defeat of the tsarist government, which led to the weakening of tsarism and the strengthening of the revolution. Trotsky, along with Mensheviks, led the treasonous policy of curtailment of the Revolution of 1904–7. Trotsky led the fight against the Leninist theory of the socialist revolution. Denying the hegemony of the proletariat in the bourgeois-democratic revolution, he denied the possibility of an alliance between the proletariat and the peasantry. Thus, Trotsky even denied the victory of the socialist revolution, the victory of the dictatorship of the proletariat. Defending the counterrevolutionary Menshevik theory of "permanent revolution," Trotsky did not believe in the strength and ability of the Russian proletariat and the revolutionary possibilities of a peasant movement; he claimed that the peasants were a class hostile to the proletariat.

In the years of the Stolypin reaction, Trotsky supported the Menshevik "liquidators," aiming to dissolve the RSDRP [Russian Social-Democratic Revolutionary Party]. Being a "centrist," Trotsky tried to reconcile and to unite the Bolsheviks and the liquidators on a liquidators' platform. Characterizing the position of Trotsky, Lenin wrote: "Trotsky conducted himself like the worst sort of careerist and factionalist . . . he prattles on about the party, but conducts himself as the worst factionalist of all." (Lenin Anthology XXV, page 38). In these very years Lenin called Trotsky "Judas-Trotsky." In 1912 Trotsky organized the anti-party "August bloc," uniting all anti-Bolshevik groups and movements against Lenin and the Bolshevik Party. Trotsky and the Trotskyites occupied on all fundamental questions the liquidators' position, but concealed their liquidationism as conciliation. Exposed by Lenin and Stalin, the Trotskyite "August bloc" disintegrated under the blows of the Bolsheviks in 1913–14.

In the period of the First World War, Trotsky in all important questions of socialism and war led the struggle against Lenin and against the Bolshevik Party. Trotskyites defended admitted social-chauvinists, called for the renunciation of the class struggle in time of war, supported the imperialist war, concealing their treason against the proletariat and socialism with "left" phraseology about the struggle with war, planning the deception of the working class. Slipping by means of deception into the ranks of the Bolshevik Party in 1917 with the purpose of undermining and blasting it from within, Trotsky organized an antiparty counterrevolutionary group of Trotskyites, speaking out against the Bolshevik Party and its leaders—Lenin and Stalin—on all fundamental questions of Marxism-Leninism and the revolution.

In the period of the preparation and carrying out of the October Socialist Revolution (April 1917–1918), Trotsky along with other traitors to the party—Zinoviev, Kamanev, Rykov, Bukharin, Pyatakov—tried by treacherous means to thwart the armed rebellion and turn the Bolshevik Party from the path to socialist revolution.

In February 1918 the Trotskyite-Bukharinite band of traitors wrecked the peace talks at Brest-Litovsk with Germany, aiming to place the as-yet unorganized Soviet Republic, lacking a strong army, under the deadly blow of

German imperialism. The treason of Trotsky and Bukharin cost the Soviet state dearly. The new terms of peace were significantly more onerous than before. Latvia, Estonia, and Lithuania went to Germany. The Ukraine was turned into a German puppet state. The Soviet Republic was required to pay an indemnity to the Germans. Lenin noted that Bukharin and Trotsky "in [this] matter aided the German imperialists and hindered the growth and development of revolution in Germany" (Lenin, Collected Works, vol. XXII, p. 307).

In the years of the foreign military intervention and civil war (1918–20) Trotsky and the Trotskyites treacherously disorganized work in the Red Army, attempting to weaken its fighting power; as saboteurs, they disrupted the fighting successes of the Red Army, giving direct help to interventionists and bourgeois-landowner counterrevolutionaries.

In the period of transition to peacetime work on restoration of the nation's economy (1921–1925) Trotsky at the head of all anti-party elements led a bitter fight against the Party of Lenin and its leaders Lenin and Stalin, who were successfully leading the Soviet country to socialism by way of the New Economic Policy. In 1923 the Trotskyites, attempting to split the party, demanded a party-wide debate, in which they were utterly defeated throughout the Soviet Union. The Thirteenth Party Conference and the Thirteenth Party Congress RKP(b) (1924) condemned the Trotskyite opposition as an openly-expressed petty-bourgeois deviation from Marxism, as revisionism of Leninism. In 1927 Trotsky in his slanderous article "The Lessons of October" attempted to replace Leninism with Trotskyism. Stalin demonstrated in his speeches that the ideological defeat of Trotsky was an indispensable condition to secure the further victorious movement towards socialism, and he rallied the party around the Central Committee for the struggle for the victory of socialism. In 1925 the Trotskyites came out against the teaching of Lenin and Stalin about the victory of socialism in the Soviet land, against the party course on the victorious construction of socialism in the USSR, and against the socialist industrialization of the country. To the general party line, to the Stalinist plan of socialist industrialization of the country, the Trotskyites offered in opposition a bourgeois plan of enslavement of the USSR, converting the Soviet Union into a feeble agrarian appendage of the capitalist world, disarmed and deprived of a possibility for existence in conditions of capitalist encirclement. The Trotskyites tried to corrupt and break up the Bolshevik Party after the death of Lenin, to infect it with their disbelief in the cause of victory of socialism in the USSR and to create a party of capitalist restoration.

In the years of struggle for socialist industrialization of the country (1926–29), the Trotskyites continued a treasonable struggle against the Party of Lenin and Stalin. In 1926, Trotsky organized the anti-party, counterrevolutionary Trotskyite-Zinovievite bloc, developing subversive work against the Bolshevist Party and Soviet government. Under the leadership of Stalin, the Party of Bolsheviks ideologically smashed and organizationally crushed the Trotskyite-Zinovievite bloc. At the Fifteenth Congress of the ACP(b) (1927) the Trotskyites and Zinovievites were expelled from the Bolshevist Party for counterrevolutionary activity. "Being ideologically smashed from the Bolshevist Party, losing any base in the working class, the Trotskyites ceased to be a political tendency and turned into an unprincipled, careerist clique of political swindlers, into a band of political double-dealers." [*History of the ACP (b), Short Course,* pp. 285–286]. In 1929, Trotsky was deported from the territory of the USSR for anti-Soviet and counterrevolutionary activity. Overseas, he continued a treasonable struggle against the Party of Lenin and Stalin and the Soviet government.

In 1932–33, Trotskyites and Bukharinites organized the anti-Soviet "Right-Trotskyite bloc." Trials in 1936, 1937, and 1938 revealed, that Bukharinites and Trotskyites headed by Trotsky, Bukharin, Zinoviev, Kamenev, and Rykov already from the first days of the Great October Socialist Revolution took part in a conspiracy against Lenin, against the Party of the Bolsheviks, against the Soviet government; long ago they had already formed one common band of the worst enemies of the people. They tried to break the Brest peace, together with "Left" SRs [Socialist Revolutionaries] overthrow Soviet authority, arrest and kill V. I. Lenin, I. V. Stalin, Ya. M. Sverdlov, and form a new government of Trotskyites, Bukharinites, and "Left" SRs. They organized the despicable wounding of Lenin in the summer of 1918; prepared the anti-Soviet rebellion of "Left" SRs in the summer of 1918; deliberately aggravated disagreements in the party in 1921, trying to loosen and overthrow from within the leadership of Lenin; they tried to overthrow the leadership of the party during Lenin's illness and after his death. The Trotskyites and Bukharinites long before this moved into the service of foreign intelligence agencies, handed over state secrets and provided foreign intelligence agencies with espionage information; carried out wrecking, sabotage, explosions; organized the despicable murders of Kirov, Menshinsky, Kuybyshev, and Gorki. Judicial proceedings revealed, that Trotsky-Bukharinite traitors, carrying out the will of their masters—foreign bourgeois intelligence agencies - set as their goal the destruction of the Bolshevik Party and the Soviet state, the undermining of the defense of the country, the facilitation of foreign military intervention, the preparation of the defeat of the Red Army, the partition of the USSR, the destruction of the gains of the workers and peasants and the restoration of capitalist slavery in the Soviet Union. For these monstrous crimes, according to the sentence of the Military Collegium of the Supreme Court of the USSR, the Bukharin-Trotskyite traitors were shot. The Soviet people approved the crushing of the counterrevolutionary "Right-Trotskyite Bloc" and rallied ever more closely around the Party of Lenin and Stalin. Trotsky was killed in 1940 by one of his [own] accomplices. Trotsky is the worst enemy of all toiling humanity; Trotskyites everywhere play the role of provocateurs and spies of the counterrevolutionary bourgeoisie in the working-class movement, trying to demoralize the Communist movement.

Glossary of Names and Titles

Collective Farm

A collective farm (kolkhoz) was a community of farmers in a stated area that included a store, a school, a library, a hospital and a clubhouse. It was created by combining small farms into one farm. The average size of a collective farm was 5,900 hectares (14,573 acres). The land used by the farm belonged to the State, and it was leased to the collective in perpetuity. Theoretically, it was a self-financed cooperative venture carried out by its members but in fact it was governed by the State's regulations, a rural soviet and district officials. The members of a collective elected the farm's managing committee and a chairman. The farm chairman was usually a Party member, and he was nominated by the Party. It was the chairman who oversaw the production of goods to meet the production goals determined by the State's planning boards. He was also to provide ideological leadership for the members of the farm. The chairman that did not meet ideological purity requirements was removed.

Komsomol

Membership in the Komsomol (The Young Communist League) was less extensive than in the Young Pioneers. Only about one-third of the young people between the ages of fifteen and twenty-eight became members. However, Komsomol membership among students in institutions of higher learning was usually high because membership helped a person gain admission into these institutions. Although the age limit for membership was twenty-eight, provision was made in the Komsomol statutes for officers to remain in the organization beyond that age.

Komsomol members were exposed to intense ideological indoctrination and were expected to participate in all aspects of Soviet society. Members would offer their services to the armed forces if the State called for recruits in an emergency situation. They were also expected to work in a factory or on a collective farm whenever there was a shortage of labor. Members who entered the military or who joined an industrial or agricultural force were responsible for the political education of their co-workers who were of the same age group. Members had been trained for this responsibility during Komsomol meetings, which were mainly discussions and lectures on Marxist-Leninist ideology.

Komsomol members performed an important surveillance function in society. They frequently inspected enterprises and did this usually without prior warning. They sought to expose corruption, waste and inefficiency in management and laziness and tardiness among workers. The surveillance function of the Komsomol was even more extensive in institutions of higher learning. The activities of students who were members were carefully observed. Failure to conform to Komsomol standards of behavior could result in expulsion from the organization. Komsomol members with a university education were an important source of recruitment for the Communist Party. Membership in the Komsomol did not, however, ensure that a person would be admitted to the Party.

October Revolution

Vladimir Lenin and his Bolsheviks removed from power the Provisional Government on November 7, 1917, according to the Gregorian calendar. The removal was called the October Revolution. In Russia the Gregorian calendar was accepted after the October Revolution (so named because it took place in October 1917 in the Julian calendar). On January 24, 1918, the Council of People's Commissars decreed that January 32, 1918, was to be followed by February 14, 1918.

Order of Lenin

The Order of Lenin was named after Vladimir Lenin. It was the highest decoration bestowed in the Soviet Union. The order was awarded to the following:

- civilians for outstanding services rendered to the State,
- members of the armed forces for exemplary service,
- those who promoted friendship and cooperation between peoples and in the strengthening of peace.

It was also bestowed on cities, companies, factories, regions, educational institutions, military units and ships. The order was established by the Central Executive Committee in April of 1930.

Order of the Red Banner

The Order of the Red Banner was the first Soviet military decoration. The order was established on September 16, 1918, during the Russian Civil War, by decree of the All-Russian Central Executive Committee. It was the highest award of Soviet Russia and subsequently the Soviet Union, until the Order of Lenin which was established in 1930.

Pravda

Pravda was a leading newspaper of the Soviet Union and an official organ of the Central Committee of the Communist Party. *Pravda* (the name means "truth" in Russian) was first issued on May 5, 1912, in St. Petersburg by the Bolshevik faction of the Marxist Social Democratic Party. Those running the newspaper wanted to publicize labor activism and expose the working conditions in Russia's factories. The editors published many letters and articles written by workers.

Pravda was subject to censorship by the tsarist authorities. These authorities had the power to fine the paper, withdraw its publication license, confiscate a specific issue, or jail the editor or editors. The paper was closed down eight times in the first two years of its existence and each time the Bolsheviks would reopen it under another name such as *Worker's Truth* or *Labor's Truth.*

From December 1917 until the summer of 1928, the paper was run by editor- in-chief Nikolai Bukharin and Maria Ilichua Ulyanova, Vladimir Lenin's sister. When Bukharin disagreed with Joseph Stalin over collectivization, Bukharin and his supporters, including Lenin's sister, were formally removed in 1929 from the editorial staff. By 1933, the paper, now headed by Lev Mukhlis, was Stalin's mouthpiece. The offices of the paper were in Moscow. (They had been transferred to Moscow on March 3, 1918, when the Soviet capital was moved there.)

Pravda was distributed throughout the Soviet Union. It offered its readers well-written articles on topics in areas such as science, economics and literature. It included articles that were meant to indoctrinate readers and inform them on Communist theory and State programs. The editors sought to create unity of thought on the part of its readers by emphasizing the Communist Party line. They published letters from readers and editorials. Many of the editorials were reprinted in other Soviet Union papers.

Pugachev, Emelyan

Emelyan Pugachev's revolt took place during the reign of Catherine II who was also known as "the Great." Pugachev (1726–75) was a Cossack who in his youth had been a military adventurer. Disappointed in his career, he made his way to the Ural Mountains where he recruited tribesmen and laborers who were being forced to work in the mines.

In 1773, Pugachev proclaimed that he was Tsar Peter III, the murdered husband of Catherine II. Pugachev claimed that he had escaped the clutches of Catherine and was resolved to give the peasants liberty from serfdom and ownership of land. He began his uprising with small raiding parties against local landlords and military outposts and soon gained the allegiance of thousands of peasants.

In 1774, with an army of nearly twenty thousand people, Pugachev captured the city of Kazan and threatened to advance on Moscow. It was another year before Catherine the Great's forces crushed the rebellion. Pugachev was captured, was brought to Moscow and was executed.

Siege of Leningrad

In June 1941, Germany's military forces invaded the Soviet Union from the west and in the following month Finland's troops advanced into Soviet territory from the north. By the end of September, the Germans and Finns had established a blockade against the city of Leningrad. Thereafter, the Germans struck the besieged city with incessant aerial bombing and with artillery fire from long-range guns. The bombs and the artillery shells caused the pipes of Leningrad's water system to burst, and the rivers that flowed through Leningrad and the city's canals became the people's sources of water. A shortage of fuel in the city reduced the power supply, adversely affecting heating, lighting and cooking. But what was most devastating was the shortage of food. Supplies were airlifted into Leningrad and delivered on barges across Lake Ladoga located east of the city, but they were insufficient to feed the people. During the last days of November and throughout most of December the daily ration of bread was 250 grams for workers in factories and 125 grams for office workers, dependents and children. People ate whatever they could find to stay alive.

The winter of 1941–1942 was particularly severe and one of the coldest in many years. The freezing temperatures, however, deepened the ice that covered Lake Ladoga and made it possible to create ice roads across the lake. Food and other supplies were brought from the Russian mainland to the east shore of the lake, transported across the lake on ice roads and then taken into Leningrad. The Road of Life, as it was called, saved the city. Yet hundreds of thousands of its people would die from starvation during the first winter of the siege.

The blockade around the city finally came to an end in early 1944. By that time more than a million Leningraders had lost their lives.

Simonov, Konstantin

Born Mikhailovich Simonov in St. Petersburg in 1915, Konstantin wrote his first poem in 1935. By 1940, he had changed his name and established himself as both a poet and dramatist. At the outbreak of the Great Patriotic War, he was posted with the army and worked on the newspaper *Red Star*. In 1941, he wrote his poem *Wait For Me* about a soldier who asks his sweetheart to wait for his return. The poem was published by *Pravda* in February 1942 and immediately won the hearts of the Soviet soldiers. They memorized it and copied it and sent it back in letters to their loved ones. The poem would help make Simonov famous in the Soviet Union.

Simonov's most well known piece of war-time fiction was a short novel entitled *Days and Nights*. It was set in Stalingrad in the dark days of late 1942 and tells the story of a Red Army military officer and his soldiers defending three apartment buildings for seventy days. With the Germans only 60 meters away, they fight on in the rain and snow and icy cold. They endure daily bombardments, tank attacks and hand-to-hand combat. They do this to hold onto three insignificant buildings (the rubble of three buildings) which to them represent all of Russia. They suffer casualties; they demonstrate extraordinary bravery, and they are awarded many medals including the Order of Lenin. The novel ends just as the long-awaited Soviet counter offensive begins to turn the tide in November 1942.

Soviet Rehabilitation

The term "rehabilitation" in the Soviet Union referred to the political and social restoration of a person who had been repressed or criminally prosecuted without due basis. "Rehabilitation" restored the person to the state of acquittal. In many cases, "rehabilitation" was posthumous, as thousands of victims had been executed or had died in prison labor camps.

Soviet Secret Police

After coming to power in Russia in 1917, the Bolsheviks relied on a strong secret police force or security force to support and protect their regime. On December 4, 1917, a Special Commission for the Fight Against Counterrevolution was set up, and on December 20 this was renamed the All-Russian Extraordinary Commission to Fight Counterrevolution and Sabotage (Vserossiskaya Chrezvychainaya Komissia Po Borbe s Konterrevoliutsiei i Sabotazhem). This organization was headed by Felix Dzerzhinsky, was attached to the Council of People's Commissars and was nominally subordinate to it. It became known as the CHEKA, from the initials of the Russian words for Extraordinary Commission. The long-drawn-out Russian Civil War helped strengthen the power of the CHEKA and encouraged the tendency for it to act in its own right and throw off any control by a governmental body. The CHEKA became, in due course, an independent body.

With the end of the Russian Civil War, the CHEKA was reorganized into the so-called State Political Administration (Gosudarstrennoe Politicheskoe Upravlenie, that is, the GPU). The GPU was entrusted with, among other tasks, the suppression of counterrevolutionary activity, the protection of the country against spies, the political protection of the frontiers and the carrying out of any special instructions from the highest government organs (the Central Committee of the Communist Party and the Council of People's Commissars). In 1923 the Unified State Political Administration (Obedinyonnoe Gosudarstvennoe Politicheskoe Upravlenie sometimes referred to as the OGPU) was created. During its tenure, which ended in 1934, repression against the Soviet citizens lessened.

In 1934 the People's Commissariat of Internal Affairs (Narodnyy Komissariat Vnutrennikh Del), better known as NKVD, was set up and the OGPU was merged in it. The NKVD was the direct instrument of Joseph Stalin for use against people in the Communist Party and against the Soviet citizens who were not members of the Party. Stalin had decided to purge the Party and the country at large. The purging became known as the Great Terror or the Great Purge. According to NKVD files, during the worst years of the Great Purge, 1937–1938, at least one and a half million people were arrested and the great majority on political charges. During the same years, some 680,000 people were sentenced to death for participating in counterrevolutionary activities and for committing State crimes.

In February 1941, it was decided to detach certain intelligence and secret police functions from the NKVD and thus the People's Commissariat for State Security (Narodnyy Komissariat Gosudarstvennoe Bezopasnosti), better known as NKGB, was formed. But several months later with the outbreak of the Great Patriotic War, the two commissariats, the NKVD and the NKGB, were reintegrated.

In 1946 all the People's Commissariats were renamed Ministries. Consequently, the NKVD was renamed the Ministry for Internal Affairs (Ministerstvo Vnutrennikh Del) or MVD and the NKGB was renamed Ministry for State Security (Ministerstvo Gosudarstvennoe Beszopasnosti) or MGB.

The MGB was held responsible for the security of the Soviet Union. It inherited the secret police functions of the old NKVD, conducting espionage and counterespionage, as well as enacting a policy of supervision and surveillance to maintain control over the Soviet citizenry and to prevent disloyalty. It directed espionage networks at home and abroad and organized both domestic and foreign counterintelligence. It was responsible for enforcing security regulations, monitoring and censoring information leaving or coming into the country and supervising the vast majority of Soviet life. The latter included the planting and organizing of agents to track and monitor public opinion and loyalty as well as ensuring the safety of important government and Communist Party officials.

The MGB was given a high level of autonomy as the agency was responsible only to the Central Committee of the Communist Party. MGB agents had the power to arrest and sentence people suspected of political crimes, including espionage. During Stalin's last years, between 1945 and 1953, more than 750,000 Soviet citizens were arrested and punished. Many of the arrests made by the MGB were founded on fabricated evidence, most notably on the suspicion of espionage.

On March 6, 1953, the day after Stalin died, the MGB and the MVD were united into one body, the MVD. On March 13, 1954, the MVD was split up. The MVD retained its traditional policing and internal security functions while the newly created Committee for State Security (Komitet Gosudarstvennoy Bezopasnosti), better known by its acronym KGB, was given the following responsibilities: overseeing foreign intelligence operations, protecting the country's political leadership, supervising the border troops and directing a general surveillance of the population.

Union of Soviet Writers

The Union of Soviet Writers was formed by the Central Committee of the Communist Party on April 23, 1932. All other literary organizations such as the All-Russian Association of Proletarian Writers were dissolved. Writers who did not belong to the official union found it almost impossible to get their work published.

In 1934, the Union of Soviet Writers adopted the doctrine of Socialist Realism. Approved by Joseph Stalin, Nickolai Bukharin, Maxim Gorky and Andrey Zhdanow, the doctrine demanded that the fine arts must depict some aspect of humankind's struggle toward socialist progress for a better life. It stressed the need for the creative artist to serve the proletariat by being realistic, optimistic and heroic. Those who believed in the doctrine, considered all forms of experimentation as degenerate and pessimistic.

The doctrine of Socialist Realism was propagated by the union's newspaper, *The Literary Gazette*. If writers rebelled against the doctrine of Socialist Realism, their work was criticized in the newspaper. If writers did not conform, they were denounced and then expelled from the union.

Young Pioneers

Within the framework of the educational system, students in the Soviet Union joined youth organizations that were sanctioned by the Communist Party. These organizations included the Young Octoberists for children between the ages of six and nine and the Young Pioneers for children between the ages of nine and fifteen. Each school had a staff member who was to administer the activities of the Young Pioneers. Each class was a detachment of Young Pioneers that was comprised of three to five units, and the detachment was led by a Komsomol member. The leaders of the Young Pioneers worked closely with the classroom teachers to teach the children to be conscientious students and good citizens.

Nearly all recreational activities for the Young Pioneers took place under the auspices of the organization. The programs that the organization sponsored ranged from sports to scouting activities to folk dancing and ballet lessons. Most communities had facilities for these activities and there were Young Pioneer camps throughout the country. Young Pioneers were exposed to ideological indoctrination, but it was usually limited to instilling patriotism and Soviet values. Intensive ideological indoctrination was reserved for the members of the Komsomol.

Bibliography

Brown, Edward J. Russian Literature since the Revolution. Cambridge, Massachusetts: Harvard University Press, 1982.

Carleton, Gregory. The Politics of Reception: Critical Constructions of Mikhail Zoshchenko. Evanston, Illinois: Northwestern University Press, 1998.

Chew, Allen F. An Atlas of Russian History: Eleven Centuries of Changing Borders. New Haven: Yale University Press, 1976.

Deutscher, I. Stalin: A Political Biography. Oxford, England: Oxford University Press, 1949.

Fischer, Louis, ed. Thirteen Who Fled. New York: Harper and Brothers, 1949.

Goure, Leon. The Siege of Leningrad. Stanford, California: Stanford University Press, 1962.

Herzl, Theodor.The Jewish State. New York: American Zionist Emergency Council, 1946.

Hosking, Geoffrey. Russia and the Russians: A History. Cambridge, Massachusetts: Harvard University Press, 2001.

Pohl, J. Otto. Ethnic Cleansing in the USSR, 1937–1949. Westport, Connecticut: Greenwood Press, 1999.

Pravda. January 28, 1949.

Pravda. February 28, 1949.

Pravda. November 26, 1924.

Pravda. January 13, 1953.

Руханен, Урхо. В вихрях века [In Whirlwinds of the Century]. Петрозаводск, Карелия, 1987.

Riasanovsky, Nicholas V. A History of Russia. London: Oxford University Press, 1969.

Sixsmith, Martin. Russia: A 1,000-Year Chronicle of the Wild East. New York: The Overlook Press, 2014.

Serge,Victor, and Natalia Sedova Trotsky. The Life and Death of Leon Trotsky.Translated by Arnold J. Pomerans. Chicago, Illinois: Haymarket Books, 2015.

Stalin, Joseph. Leninism. Vol. II. New York: International Publishers, 1933.

Trotsky, Leon. My Life: An Attempt at an Autobiography. New York: Pathfinder Press, Inc., 1970.

Index

About the Authors

Alexey Vinogradov earned his Ph.D. in archaeology at Leningrad State University. He is the acting chairman of the Research Center for Archaeology, Historical Sociology, and Cultural Heritage of the St. Petersburg State University in St. Petersburg, Russia.

Albert Pleysier was born in Utrecht, the Netherlands. He earned his Ph.D. in European history from West Virginia University and is currently a professor of history at Piedmont College in Demorest, Georgia.

Books by the Authors

Bitva za Leningrad v sud' bakh zhitelel goroda I oblasti: vospominahiiy a zashchitnikov I zhitelei blokadnogo goroda I okkupirovan-nykh territorii (*The Battle of Leningrad: Memories of its Citizens and People in the Occupied Surrounding Areas*)
Saint Petersburg State University Press, 2005

Surviving the Blockade of Leningrad
University Press of America, 2006

The Women of Ismaelovka: A Soviet Union Collective Farm in Siberia
University Press of America, 2007

Frozen Tears: The Blockade and Battle of Leningrad
University Press of America, 2008

Unlocked Memories: Young Russians under German Rule
University Press of America, 2011

Henry VIII and the Anabaptists
University Press of America, 2014

Lightning Source UK Ltd.
Milton Keynes UK
UKHW040615300119
336452UK00001B/4/P

9 780761 870395